You've Been SET UP

Mary June Collins

You've Been Set Up
© 2010 by Mary June Collins

Published by Insight Publishing Group
8801 S. Yale, Suite 410
Tulsa, OK 74137
918-493-1718

All rights reserved. No part of this book may be reproduced or transmitted in any form or by any means, electronic or mechanical, including photocopying and recording, or by an information storage and retrieval system, without permission in writing from the author.

Unless otherwise noted all Scripture quotations are taken from the *New International Version,* © 1960, 1962, 1963, 1968, 1971, 1973, 1975, 1977, 1995 by the Lockman Foundation. Used by permission.

Scripture quotations marked NKJV are taken from the Holy Bible, *New King James Version,* © 1979, 1980, 1982 by Thomas Nelson, Inc., Publishers.

Scripture quotations marked KJV are from the Holy Bible: King James Version.

Scripture quotations marked NLT are from the *New Living Translation,* © 1996. Used by permission of Tyndale House Publishers, Inc. Wheaton, Illinois 60189. All rights reserved.

ISBN: 978-1-932503-87-6
Library of Congress catalog card number: 2010920425

Printed in Canada

DEDICATION

To my wonderful husband, Dennis. Thank you for always loving me unconditionally, encouraging me, and praying for me. You are my hero, my best friend, my partner, and lover.

To my precious children—Kelli and Jason, Jason and Amanda, Cory and Juliane, Patrick and Breeanna, Kyle and Lacey. I love and adore you. You have given me life's greatest memories and a future of happiness.

To my awesome grandchildren—Christian, Katy, Matthew, and Logan. You make me laugh and keep me young. You are a shining example of God's love and living proof of the generational blessing of increase and joy!

CONTENTS

Acknowledgments...7
Chapter One: My Kids Will Never Forget This Day.................9
Chapter Two: Your Setup...17
Chapter Three: Time Is On Your Side..................................29
Chapter Four: Divine Intervention.......................................37
Chapter Five: What You See Is What You Get.....................45
Chapter Six: Do You Have a Heart Condition?....................53
Chapter Seven: Life Isn't Fair but God Is.............................61
Chapter Eight: Choices Are Simple So Don't Make Them Difficult......69
Chapter Nine: Top Ten Choices Before You.........................77
Chapter Ten: Your Spiritual GPS..83
Chapter Eleven: Let Favor Work For You.............................91
Chapter Twelve: Send Out Some Good Vibrations.............101
Chapter Thirteen: What My Friend the Rattlesnake Taught Me......109
Chapter Fourteen: Speak Up!...117
Chapter Fifteen: Divine Connections..................................127
Chapter Sixteen: The Amazing Power of Belief..................133
Chapter Seventeen: Bloom Where You Are Planted..........141
Chapter Eighteen: Love Connection...................................149
Chapter Nineteen: Grace, Amazing Grace..........................159
Chapter Twenty: Crazy Love..169
Chapter Twenty-One: When Turbulence Hits....................177
Chapter Twenty-Two: A Familiar Voice.............................185
Chapter Twenty-Three: The Passion Play..........................191
Chapter Twenty-Four: Your Best Is Yet to Come...............195
Chapter Twenty-Five: The Greatest Setup.........................203

ACKNOWLEDGMENTS

Every accomplishment is a result of what we have learned from all who have been a part of our lives, both directly and indirectly.

I am forever grateful for my pastors, Drs. Tom and Maureen Anderson. They have faithfully taught me the uncompromised Word of God. They have walked the walk they teach, which has spoken volumes of silent truth to my life. They have been there for me in the darkest of times to speak faith and truth into my life. I wouldn't have a book to write today if it wasn't for their mentorship in my life.

I humbly extend gratitude to my book coach, John Mason, of Insight Publishing Group. Thank you for believing in me and patiently guiding me through this amazing experience. You kept me moving forward and equipped me to get to the finish line.

Much love and gratefulness to my Savior, Jesus Christ. Thank you for giving me your Holy Spirit who is the true author of this book. Not one word could have been written without your guidance. Thank you for having something to say through me and using me to bring your truth and glory into this world. My message does not come with wise and persuasive words, but with a demonstration of your power. All glory to you!

CHAPTER ONE

My Kids Will Never Forget This Day

One Sunday morning at church, our youth pastor took the pulpit. Excitedly announcing summer youth camp, he made it sound like so much fun for my kids! I knew it would be a life-changing experience for them spiritually. My heart's desire was to send my three oldest children.

On the way home, I mentioned it to my husband. He certainly was for it, but was concerned about the cost. We lived on a pretty tight budget at the time and anything extra was a challenge. Under my breath, I prayed a short prayer that included: "Lord, I know you make a way where there seems to be no way. You meet all of our needs."

The next part sounds like a fairy tale but it is the absolute truth. As we pulled into the driveway, my husband saw something in the side yard. He got out of the car and walked over to find a crisp one-hundred-dollar bill on the lawn.

Thrilled, Dennis hollered at all of us as we walked into the house. "Hey! I just found a one-hundred-dollar bill! Come out here and look around. You might find more."

The kids ran over to him, scouting the area. They ended up finding over three hundred dollars. Unbelievable!

My kids will never forget that day. I know they looked for money in the yard every day for months after that. Money from heaven!

To this day we don't know how the money got there, but I knew that God answered my prayer. Kelli, Jason, and Cory went to youth camp that summer. God supernaturally provided the money. He must have really wanted them there.

See the setup? God put the desire in my heart to send my children to church camp. Then he prompted me to pray the Word to meet the need. I remember praying, "God, you meet all of our needs according to your riches in glory."

As a result, God caused the miraculous to happen. That's how it works every time. I didn't expect it to happen that fast or that way. God has a sense of humor and he always surprises me.

God doesn't always work as quickly as that, but he will meet your need. God has the perfect timing for all things. He honors his Word expressed in the prayer of faith.

Here is another story that unfolds an amazing setup. It's a true story about a mother who got a multimillion-dollar idea while watching her children play during summer vacation.

While playing outside, Sheri glanced over to see one of her children sticking flowers into the holes of her Crocs shoes. "What a great idea!" she thought. "In fact," she told herself, "that would be a fun craft." A few days later, Sheri went on a material-finding hunt to make charms for all of her children's Croc shoes.

When Sheri's entrepreneurial-minded husband came home and saw the pile of decked-out Crocs, he thought, "This is an amazing idea that could really turn into something big." His wheels started turning.

My Kids Will Never Forget This Day

That night, Sheri and her husband wrote the beginning plans for their new business.

Sheri went from being a full-time mom to simultaneously running a business. She and her husband turned their basement into a workshop and Sheri spent a good portion of her day making what she called Jibbitz. Hearts, flowers, butterflies, and happy faces were glued onto cuff links and then fastened into the holes of the shoes.

In a short amount of time, Sheri was receiving 250 orders a day from their Web site. Within one year, Jibbitz charms were offered in thousands of stores, and over eight million pieces had been sold worldwide.

One day when Sheri was busy working, her dad decided to take her kids to the swimming pool. Wearing their decked-out shoes, they caught the attention of none other than Crocs' cofounder Lyndon "Duke" Hanson. He was dazzled by the idea. Handing his business card to one of the children, he said, "Please have your mom call me."

You guessed it; Crocs, Inc. scooped up Jibbitz, LLC for ten million dollars. In less than a year and a half, Sheri and her family became rich and famous.[1]

Sheri Schmelzer was set up for success. What Sheri thought of as a fun craft idea turned into destiny.

What are the odds of her children running into the cofounder of Crocs at the pool? Sheri was destined to become a very successful wife, mom, entrepreneur, and mentor. Another by-product of her success is the number of women who e-mail her for advice. Sheri is quick to tell them, "You can't always have certainty, sometimes you just need to jump. Close your eyes and take a leap of faith and hope that it all works out in the end."[2]

> *Your unbelievable life story has already been written, with God as the author.*

God has placed seeds of greatness within you that define your purpose. Your passion gives you the potential to make it big. Your unbelievable life story has already been written, with God as the author.

Maybe it's hard for you to believe that your setup is as amazing and as successful as Sheri's. You may think she just had good luck and you've never been lucky. Or you are not smart enough, good enough, or talented enough.

Whatever you're tempted to think right now, if it's negative or full of excuses, take those thoughts captive and become open minded to what God wants to speak to you through this book.

The apostle Paul declares, " 'No eye has seen, no ear has heard, no mind has conceived, what God has prepared for those who love him,'—but God has revealed it to us by his Spirit" (1 Cor. 2:9-10).

Get ready! The Spirit of God is going to reveal to you your setup. You've just got to get started.

> *Start something. Start somewhere. Start now!*
>
>

Start something. Start somewhere. Start now! Do not despise small beginnings. Little by little, you will make progress and learn from your mistakes.

Stick your neck out there in faith and look for what you cannot see. Don't be shortsighted. Don't allow other people to rain on your parade. Don't let your negative past paralyze your future. God is going "to bat" for you. Don't miss the home run.

You are about to give birth to new dreams and visions for your life. You are going to realize you're set up and start living it. What God spoke about your life when he created you is out there working for you. His Word is the power making it happen.

Your destiny has been God breathed and is full of his nature and ability. As you yield yourself into his hands—acknowledging his will for your life—

My Kids Will Never Forget This Day

you will begin to see the signs of his divine intervention. Then you will step in tune with your destiny and start moving in the right direction.

Just like Sheri, things will happen to you that will make your jaw drop. You will be at the right place at the right time. You will meet that mate that you have prayed for. You will get that promotion that didn't seem possible. You will find your self-esteem rising to a higher level and a flame of courage emerging from within.

When you allow God to direct your footsteps, you will walk right into your setup. You will walk in ways of wisdom and your life will be sweet.

King Solomon, the wisest man who ever lived, passed on his godly father's words about partnering with our all-wise God: "Listen, my son, accept what I say, and the years of your life will be many. I guide you in the way of wisdom and lead you along straight paths. When you walk, your steps will not be hampered; when you run, you will not stumble" (Prov. 4:10-12).

His path will take you places you've never dreamed of. You will accomplish things you never thought were possible. "The path of the righteous is like the first gleam of dawn, shining ever brighter till the full light of day" (Prov. 4:18).

Your life was designed to bring light and life into the world. You are a life changer and a history maker. You are no different than Sheri. She is an ordinary person who did the extraordinary because she followed her heart right into her setup.

Sheri and her husband decided to take a risk. Why not? What could they lose? They took advantage of their God-given abilities and talents, expecting success. They dared to believe they could do it.

Belief is an attitude that draws the inevitable to you. Sheri and her husband

> *Belief is an attitude that draws the inevitable to you.*

stepped into the rhythm of life that God set in place for them when he created them.

It is time for you to discover who God made you to be. This book will give you the keys to unleash your destiny, enabling you to walk in the steps that have been ordered by the Lord.

Years ago, a very wealthy man and his devoted young son shared a passion for art collecting. Together they traveled around the world, adding only the finest art treasures to their collection. Priceless works by Picasso, Vincent van Gogh, Monet, and many others adorned the walls of their family estate.

The widowed, elderly man looked on with satisfaction as his only child became an experienced art collector. The son's trained eye and sharp business mind caused his father to beam with pride as they dealt with art collectors around the world.

Around this time, war engulfed the nation and the young son left to serve his country. After only a few short weeks, his father received news that his son was missing in action. Within days, it was confirmed that his son had died while rescuing a fellow soldier.

Distraught and lonely, the father went into a deep depression. The paintings on the wall continually reminded him that his son was not coming home.

One day, a uniformed visitor stood at his door. The soldier introduced himself by saying, "I was the soldier your son was saving when he died. May I come in? I want to show you something."

As the two began to talk, the soldier recalled all the conversations he'd had with the son about the love of art he shared with his dad.

Then the soldier pulled out a package and said, "I, too, am an artist and I want to give you something." The father opened the package to find a portrait of his son, featuring him in striking detail.

My Kids Will Never Forget This Day

Overcome with emotion, the father promised to hang the portrait above the fireplace. The painting became his most prized possession.

The following year, the father passed away. Since his only heir was dead, the art world waited in anticipation of an impressive art auction.

Art collectors from all over the world showed up for the auction to bid on some of the world's most spectacular paintings. The auction began with a painting that was not on any museum list. It was the painting of his son.

The auctioneer asked for an opening bid, but the room was silent. "Who will open the bidding with one hundred dollars?" he asked. Moments passed as no one spoke.

From the back of the room came, "Who cares about that painting? It's just a picture of his son. Let's forget it and get on to the good ones." More voices echoed in agreement.

"No, we have to sell this one first," replied the auctioneer. "Now who will take the son?"

Finally, a friend of the father spoke. "Will you take ten dollars for the painting? That's all I have."

"Will anyone go higher?" called the auctioneer.

After more silence he said, "Going once, going twice, gone!"

Cheers filled the room and someone shouted, "Now we can get on with the auction and bid on these treasures!"

The auctioneer looked at the audience and announced that the auction was over. Stunned disbelief quieted the room. Finally, someone asked, "What do you mean it's over? What about the millions of dollars of other paintings here?"

The auctioneer replied, "It's very simple. According to the will of the father, whoever takes the son, gets it all."[3]

What a setup! The loving father had one desire. Whoever accepted his son would be extremely blessed. He set someone up to have it all.

You've Been Set Up

Whoever would humble himself to buy the portrait of his son would be blessed forever!

Sounds like the same opportunity that God has given to you. Partner with God and you'll get it all. Your setup is waiting for you.

God has put desires in your heart. Ask him to unveil them. He has given you talents. Ask him to use them. God has set you up. Let him reveal it to you.

CHAPTER TWO
==========

Your Setup

In 1971, twenty dollars was a lot of money to us. We were newlyweds and neither one of us had a job. Dennis had just gotten out of the service and was attending college, and I had just moved back to Ohio and was looking for a job. We returned wedding gifts to pay the rent. We didn't have credit cards; we used cash for everything.

We put a twenty-dollar bill in our bedroom drawer for safekeeping. A few days later, we went back to get it and it wasn't there. We searched the whole house thinking we may have put it somewhere else, but we didn't find it. We were very upset because that was our grocery money for the week.

We had been invited to my Grandma's house for dinner that evening. That was always a big treat. She was a good cook, it was a free dinner, and we always played Crazy Eights. We loved her company.

Losing the money weighed heavily on our hearts, so we talked about it at dinner. Grandma immediately said, "You didn't lose that money. What has happened is that the twenty-dollar bill somehow got shoved behind the drawer. Take the drawer out and you will find it!"

The first thing we did when we got home was run into our bedroom and yank out the drawer. Bingo! It was there! Exactly like Grandma said, it had been pushed back behind the drawer. We were elated and relieved, knowing we had money to eat. We were so thankful for Grandma's wisdom!

That was the day I got the revelation that God cared about little ole me. I was significant in his eyes. I realized he cared about everything in my life. He would always be on my side, looking out for me. What a security I felt in his great love for me!

He felt our pain when we thought we had lost that money. He knew our need. He found a way to get that money back into our hands. If it weren't for Grandma's wisdom, we would have never found the money. Her wisdom came from God who set us up to find it.

> *Every aspect of your life has been intricately woven together by the One who created you.*
>
>

Yes, I think that was a setup. What about you? Can't you see God's hand in every detail of your daily life? When you trace your footsteps, you know that only God could be responsible for all the blessings that have come your way. Every aspect of your life has been intricately woven together by the One who created you.

Now you are about to discover the most amazing truth, known to only a select group of mankind. Only a few search and find the road to their divine destiny and live it out. Matthew states in his gospel that small is the gate and narrow the road that leads to life; and only a few find it.

This road to life is the one you've been set up to live and enjoy. It is the hidden agenda of all of your days that you were destined to live. If you hang in here with me and follow the wisdom revealed in this book, you will find your destined days. Your abundantly blessed life is about to be revealed to you.

You can't fulfill your ultimate destiny on your own. It takes a partnership with God. The Creator of your human body is also the Creator of

Your Setup

your remarkable life story. The reason for your existence is not a mystery or hidden secret. The predetermined course of the events in your life will come to light as you catch on to the fact that you've been set up.

What do I mean by that? "You've been set up" means that your life has been programmed or prearranged by God. You have been predestined to live a full, productive, satisfying, and extremely blessed life.

God has made provision for you to live free to be who he created you to be. He has

> *God has made provision for you to live free to be who he created you to be.*
>
>

set you up to know who you are and why he created you. Even more amazingly, he has organized a supernatural plan for you to walk it out.

God has prophetically designed your life. His strategic plan has been laid out in advance and awaits your move. Stop spinning your wheels doing your own thing or what others say you should be doing. Get up and go straight forward with him. Channel yourself into your God-ordained life.

Allow me to teach you how to walk right into your setup. You will know without a doubt who God made you to be and what you are called to do. You will see a clear picture for today, tomorrow, and your future. You will be able to look back on your life, connect the dots of your past, and see the plans for your future.

Isn't that exciting? Release yourself now into the hands of your Maker. The more you open yourself up to God and his infinite plan and knowledge for you, the greater your life will become. He will launch you into your divine destiny. You will join the big league of victors. Your paramount life awaits your decision.

"What does the Lord your God ask of you but to fear the Lord your God, to walk in all his ways, to love him, to serve the Lord your God with all your heart and with all your soul, and to observe the Lord's commands and decrees that I am giving you today for your own good?" (Deut 10:12-13).

At a particular point in my life, I experienced a very strong appetite to know and please God. I wanted more. "How can I get closer to God?" I thought. He seemed so far away up there in heaven.

I wondered, "Isn't there more to being a Christian? I'm not satisfied. I'm not fulfilled. I need answers! I need wisdom to raise these little children."

In constant turmoil, I cried out for more of God. I wanted to know him better. Although I was raised in church and was a regular attendee, I felt completely unfulfilled in my relationship with God.

About that time I read a book called *Clap Your Hands*. It was a story about someone having the same frustrations as I was. Always wanting more, searching for a real, intimate relationship with God. I could relate to everything written in the book because the author and I were raised in the same kind of church. All of our religious beliefs and rituals had been the same.

That book introduced me to a life filled with the Holy Spirit. In fact, I was filled with the Holy Spirit while reading that book and my life changed forever. God consumed my heart with his presence and his power. I no longer had to look up to heaven or go to church to get in touch with him.

That day I was launched into my set-up life. I had purpose, security, and direction. My desire was to do his will only. I was sold out to the One who loved me. I knew he had great things in store for me. My best life was ahead.

I believe you have this book in your hands because you've been set up just like I have been. God has already prepared your heart for this journey. He wants to lead you into the Promised Land, where every child of God

Your Setup

should live. Your birthright of blessing, goodness, victory, and abundance awaits your acceptance of it.

This book will inspire and motivate you to take possession of what is already yours. A high price was paid for your freedom and access into your inheritance. Jesus shed his blood to set you free from a life of mediocrity and bondage. God designed you to be free; free to be naturally you.

You were born to live out your dreams with purpose and passion. He has set in place everything you would ever want or need to make them happen. Nothing can compare or come close to the incredible life he has for you.

"For I know the plans I have for you," declares the Lord, "plans to prosper you and not to harm you, plans to give you hope and a future" (Jer. 29:11).

The world is waiting for you to get into position. God wants you to step up into his kingdom where there is no lack. He is forever striving to get his children to live in the Promised Land.

From Genesis to Revelation, his will is plainly written and displayed in the lives of every character in the Bible. Some of them stepped up into their call right away and did it. Others ran from their call, afraid they couldn't do it. Many didn't have a clue what their destiny was and were too busy doing their own thing. Whatever the case, God always showed up to get them back on track to do his will.

Many times, we have questioned God's will for our lives. My husband, Dennis, had been in the newspaper business for fourteen years when he was asked to transfer from Ohio to Mesa, Arizona, for a great promotion.

Both of us and our five children were born in Springfield, Ohio. Our families lived within the city limits. You could drive from one end of the city to the other in twenty minutes—no big deal. Our closest friends were people we grew up with and had known all our lives.

How could we possibly leave our loved ones and move two thousand miles away from our roots? "Where in the world is Arizona, anyway?" we asked ourselves.

At first we thought there was no way we could ever make such a drastic change. It would be so hard on our parents if we moved that far away with their five grandchildren. I was extremely close to my mother and especially didn't want to leave her. The more we thought it out, the more impossible it looked.

Even though we didn't want to leave our hometown, we started to get excited about the new adventure. In our hearts, we felt life and peace. When God impressed us to fly to Arizona and be open to this opportunity, we did.

While we were visiting, God made it very clear to us that Arizona was his plan. When we made the decision to move, our hearts were filled with joy and peace. We trusted in him and wondered what he had in store for us and our children.

The words God spoke to our hearts were "Trust in the Lord with all your heart, and lean not on your own understanding; in all your ways acknowledge Him, and He shall direct your paths" (Prov. 3:5-6 NKJV).

> *Your life is now in motion because of the words God has spoken about your life.*
>
>

Those words moved us to Arizona. Yes, Arizona was definitely God's perfect plan. We were transplanted for his purposes of which I will share many in this book.

Your life is now in motion because of the words God has spoken about your life. God set you up to do his will. He created you in your mother's womb then breathed his breath of life into your being. The destiny he spoke over your life at creation is the undeniable force that keeps you moving in the right direction. Sometimes you may fight against it or even ignore it but nothing can change his mind. You were created for his purposes and he is determined to get your attention to follow his fatherly advice.

Sometimes God's will takes us off guard. He surprises us. I often think about the apostle Paul. He was so far away from doing what God ordained him to do. Paul was killing Christians. He didn't believe in Jesus; he was an enemy of God. He was on a mission to destroy the church.

But Paul was set up to meet God through a bolt of lightning that knocked him off his feet. His natural eyes were blinded but his spiritual eyes were opened. Paul knew he had an encounter with the God of Abraham, Isaac, and Jacob.

The Truth set him free from his past and launched him into his set-up life. He was transformed by God from a persecutor of Christians to a preacher for Christ. He persuaded millions to believe in Jesus and wrote thirteen New Testament epistles.

Paul wrote, "For to me, to live is Christ and to die is gain. If I am to go on living in the body, this will mean fruitful labor for me" (Phil. 1:21-22).

In his words, we hear that the only thing worth living is the life God has ordained for you to live. It's a fruitful life. It's a blessed life.

And we know that Paul had many struggles. He was imprisoned and suffered for the sake of the Gospel. But he was the one who wrote, "In all our troubles my joy knows no bounds" (2 Cor. 7:4).

Maybe you have a great life right now. Well then, God wants to take you to the next level. He has more for you than you can ever imagine. He will increase every area of your life. Let go of your limits and dare to believe for more. He longs to give it to you.

On the contrary, maybe your life is full of problems and heartache. You've lost all hope. You can't believe you can live a life of happiness. God seems so far away. The challenges that surround you may feel overwhelming.

You could be mad at God and asking why he allowed certain things to happen to you.

If that is you, then your life is about to change dramatically. You are going to conquer those giants, those negative mindsets, those lies of the enemy. God is not the source of your problems—he's the solution.

"In this world you will have trouble. But take heart! I have overcome the world" (John 16:33).

> *God is not the source of your problems—he's the solution.*
>
>

God makes a way where there seems to be no way. He is fully capable of navigating you through the wilderness to get to the Promised Land. He will guide you where you should be and surround you with help. He is a father who leads his children into safety, security, and fullness of life.

He will heal and restore you, as well as redeem the troubles in your past. Hope is entering your heart right now. You can conquer all your fear with his power. You can do all things with his strength. Believe for the impossible to happen in your life.

Maybe you don't feel worthy to have God bless you and make you fruitful in this life. Or you don't believe it's God will to prosper his children and lavish them with blessing upon blessing.

Furthermore, you may have doubts about the idea that God has a divine plan for your existence. Maybe you have never believed in predestination.

That's OK for now. Just hang in there with me. This book provides the truth that will set you free. Give God a chance to explain his character. Your perception of him will change as you hear the truth from his Word.

You will be convinced that God is good all the time. God can never create anything bad. He is the author of life, not death. He is the source of light, not darkness. He is truth and cannot lie. He is always the same;

Your Setup

He can never change his mind. His Word (truth) can change your mind, causing your life to change too.

I spent the first thirty years of my life living to please other people. I did what I thought others thought I should do. I was a people pleaser. I thought that was a good thing.

I didn't have a clear sense of direction for my life. My thinking was, "If I'm a good person, God will lead me into good things and I will be happy." Like most people, I sailed along, catching a wave to take me wherever it was going. I was unfulfilled and unhappy.

As I explained previously, I knew God, went to church, even prayed, and God answered. But I didn't understand that he had a specific plan for my life. I had no idea that God wanted to be personally involved in every detail of my being.

After being filled with the Holy Spirit, I started to read the Bible. I began to understand God's desire for me as his child. I came across a Scripture one day that said, "All the days ordained for me were written in your book before one of them came to be" (Ps. 139:16).

It was almost as if I heard those words out loud. I couldn't stop reading that Scripture over and over again. God was speaking to me as I read his Word and he really wanted me to get it.

At that moment, I realized I was set up with a divine destiny. I cried with tears of joy because I really felt important for the first time in my life. I wasn't just a wife and a mom, a friend, a coworker, a daughter. I was purposely made to be an ambassador of almighty God.

I decided right then to walk out my God-ordained days. I said, "God, I don't want to miss out on anything you have written in your book about me. I want to do it all, experience it all, live it all—just the way you have it planned. My days are in your hands."

Since then, I have witnessed his unfailing presence and amazing direction in my life every day. God's supernatural involvement in my life has taught me to always expect the best no matter what the situation may be.

I know that his ever-increasing blessing over my life is continually setting me up to do his good and perfect will.

This God-ordained blessed life is guaranteed to all of his children. God plays no favorites. His promises are for all who believe.

God is good, all the time.

You were blessed to be a blessing, to benefit those around you. God planned your destiny by his infinite wisdom. Your life is amazing!

Join with me in believing that you were set up to read this book. You will read stories of real-life setups. Many are my own.

I made many attempts to write this book. Each time, I would get frustrated and quit. I could give you many reasons to back up my defeat, but I won't bore you with that. They were all excuses.

In 2007, some friends asked my husband, Dennis, and I to attend a business conference in Hawaii. "Why not?" we thought. "We could use a time of refreshing and motivation."

Before the very first meeting, my husband and I had an argument. I can't even remember what it was about, but I do remember being very upset with him. Sitting there thinking about our argument, I totally blocked out the first speaker. I was in the mad zone.

When we took a break, Dennis remarked about how much he enjoyed the speaker, John Mason. "Let's go meet him. He is a book coach. Maybe he can help you with your book."

Of course, I had no idea who he was talking about because I had been checked out.

From that morning until the last day of the conference, Dennis was on a mission to find John Mason. Unfortunately, he was nowhere to be found.

Your Setup

Dennis had signed up to play in a golf match on the last day. We were scheduled to fly back to Phoenix afterwards. I would pick him up at the golf course, packed and ready to go.

He came to the car smiling from ear to ear. Evidently, he'd had a great round of golf and I would hear all about it. Surprisingly, that's not what he was smiling about.

He had played golf with John Mason. They rode in the same golf cart and Dennis told him about my book. He asked him if he would coach me. Of course he said yes— he was set up!

Make this day the beginning of your journey into your God-ordained destiny. God is willing and able to reveal to you the book he wrote about your life. He wants to walk you out of the wilderness and into your Promised Land. He will take you through territories you never knew existed.

Come out of the desert. Instead of tossing to and fro and stumbling around in the darkness because you are set on doing your own thing, start living to please him. He's not going to ask you to give up anything or do something you don't want to do.

God chose you. "He chose us in him before the creation of the world to be holy and blameless in his sight. In love, he predestined us to be adopted as his sons through Jesus Christ, in accordance with his pleasure and will" (Eph 1:4-5).

He made you in his image and likeness. You have his nature and abilities. You have a free will to choose whether or not you will take advantage of what he has given to you.

If you choose to do your own thing and live your life on your own, you will forfeit his ability, his guidance, and your setup.

Challenge yourself to let God be in charge of your life. Let go of your simple ways and hop on your Daddy's back. He'll carry you off to adventures you could never imagine. He'll cause you to succeed beyond your natural ability. It is his pleasure to show you the good life and equip you to live it.

God has a supernatural way for you to achieve your dreams. He has mapped out for you a high road to success. His plan is easy, exciting, and fun.

You have seeds of his power and ability in you, ready to grow and produce great things. He will continually increase you and stretch you in every direction. He will pour out so much blessing you won't be able to contain it all. Your mouth will be filled with praise and you will say, "Look what the Lord has done!"

This book was his desire first and then it became mine. After it became mine, I gave it back to him. His desires for you are written on every page.

CHAPTER THREE

Time Is On Your Side

Though no one can go back and make a brand-new start, anyone can start now and make a brand-new ending.

Ask yourself: What baby steps can I take today to accomplish the dream I have in my heart? What is it that I can do right now that will move me closer to my aspirations? If I am going to change the direction that I am going, I need to shuffle things up and do something different.

One of our greatest fears is that we have passed up all opportunities to fulfill our destiny. The things we should have done, but didn't do, haunt us.

Thoughts like these can plague us:
- "I'll never recover from all the time I've wasted doing my own thing."
- "It's too late—I'm too old, I can't change now."
- "I'm still not sure what I'm supposed to be doing, anyway."

> *Though no one can go back and make a brand-new start, anyone can start now and make a brand-new ending.*
>
>

- "There's no way I can get into my setup at this stage of my life. It will never happen."
- "For me, time is a curse; I will never have enough of it!"

Well, applaud the devil because his lies have become more real to you than the truth. He's made a way into your brain to cause you to think this way. You've been trapped into believing his lies. Now you are under his power and headed for nowhere. He is the master of fear, doubt, and unbelief and able to lead you into a world of self-destruction.

But don't worry; we've all had the same thoughts.

I know it's hard for you to believe there is a way out of this snare. The lies of the devil make you think that you are sinking in quicksand. The longer you have believed them, the deeper you have sunk. Now you're up to your neck; you want to give up, throw in the towel. Forget the dream, it's impossible! At this point, it would be easy to do what most of us do—forfeit the big thing and go back to what's comfortable.

At one point in Dennis's and my life, it looked like we were headed for bankruptcy. Our business had been struggling for a couple of years. We were doing all that we knew to do, physically and spiritually.

Our pastors were praying with us and for us all the time. They continually encouraged us not to give up. One Saturday morning, our pastor's wife called me and asked if she could go to the business with me and pray. Sure! Whatever it took, I was for it.

Pastor Maureen showed up with a shovel and a Bible. She said, "We are planting a Bible in the front lawn of your business. This is God's property and no weapon formed against it shall prosper."

That's exactly what we did. Then we walked through the building, praying in each room and over each employee's desk. The business was saturated with prayer and agreement that God would turn it around.

Well, what do you think happened? Within six months, our business was thriving again. We were back on top and moving forward. The impossible circumstances that were against us changed. We knew only God could make those changes. He was faithful to us again.

Today, three of our sons are working the business. They have stepped up to the plate and have taken it to the next level. Years ago, if we would have given up, the inheritance would have been stolen from our children. Thank God that he always shows us the big picture and faithfully helps us achieve it.

We never go backwards in God; the kingdom of God keeps forcefully advancing. God will always move you ahead to greater things because he is a God of increase. What God has blessed cannot be cursed. It can only be missed by fear, doubt, and unbelief.

God has set you free from all the lies of the enemy. The Savior came over two thousand years ago and took every one of the devil's lies to the cross for you. You have already been set free. Somehow you just don't know it or haven't taken advantage of what Jesus has done for you.

Maybe you know it in your mind but it hasn't sunk down into your heart. If you would take the time to meditate it into your heart, you would miraculously be free.

Whom the Son sets free, is free indeed, reveals John 8:36.

Claiming your freedom in Christ will release the gift of discernment in you. The devil has no power over you any longer; you will become aware of his schemes to steal from your life and the time you have on this earth.

We're back to that word again—*time!* Let's talk about it. Why do we limit ourselves by time? Why do we always say we don't have enough time?—"I'm busy all the time. I wish I had more time! Time is running out."

You've Been Set Up

We base our whole lives around time. Time is our greatest concern. Time tells us when to eat, sleep, work, play (hopefully), and when to die. When we are controlled and manipulated by time, it has become a curse to us instead of a blessing.

Don't get mad at me; let me explain by the Word of God how and when time became a curse. Then you will understand how we subconsciously let time dictate our daily lives.

We were created in the image of God, who is an eternal, spirit being. God breathed the breath of eternal life into Adam and Eve when he created them. They were destined to live in the garden with God forever.

Before their fall, they were eternal beings. Because they did not believe God and disobeyed his Word, they received the curse of death in their bodies. Death brought time into the earth. Now, their time on earth was limited.

Minute by minute, their bodies started to decay. Before sin, they were eternal beings and living in the blessing. After sin, they were mortal beings and subject to time, living under the curse. Time became a curse.

The good news is, the curse was destroyed at the cross by the blood of Jesus. We all have a free will to choose life or death.

If we choose life, we have access to the blessings of eternity. The spirit man never dies. When our mortal bodies wear out, the spirit man moves to heaven to be with our Creator forever.

Knowing you are an eternal being changes your attitude about time and life. You are no longer in a prison of time. You now are eternally minded. You are living in the kingdom, partaking of all the blessings of heaven now and for eternity.

That is the glorious, God-given inheritance for Christians that Paul talked about, which we possess now and forever. He prayed that we would know "the riches of his glorious inheritance in the saints, and his incomparably great power for us who believe. That power is like the working of his mighty strength, which he exerted in Christ when he raised him from the dead and seated him at his right hand in the heavenly realms, far above all rule and authority, power and dominion, and every title that can be given, *not only in the present age but also in the one to come"* (Eph. 1:18-21, emphasis added).

We have dominion and power in this present age. We are blessed with a glorious inheritance on this earth. Our faith in God's Word brings it into the present. We step into a different realm—the supernatural—where we are living in eternity right now.

> *We step into a different realm—the supernatural—where we are living in eternity right now.*
>
>

Now is the time for God's glory to be manifested in the earth. Now is the time for healing, restoration, and all the promises in the Word to be fulfilled in your life. Now is the time for you to live out your setup.

Remember, you are a spirit being. Start living your life in eternity now. Since there is no time in eternity, I want you to grab ahold of the truth that you are no longer under the curse of time. Time will actually become a blessing to you. You will enjoy your time and use it respectfully. You won't live under its limitations.

The world's timetable will not order your life any longer. You will be a millionaire in your twenties and enjoy skiing in your seventies. You will step into his incomparably great power because you believe.

When God created you and your life plan, he was smart enough to give you plenty of time to carry it out. He designed your destiny from season to season with a perfect timing for everything, where you will have more than enough time in every day because you won't waste it.

In his perfect plan, God will not allow you to waste time or take it for granted. He will fill your days with work that you enjoy. You see, his plan is for you to work and have fun at the same time. That is a gift from God, and he adds no trouble to it.

But many times we feel like God is holding out on us, so we get anxious about his timing. When it looks like things are not happening fast enough, that's when we can get ourselves in trouble by giving up or getting mad. Then we lose out altogether; we were on the verge of a breakthrough, but then we lost it. Now God has to work on our hearts to get us back into a place of receiving from him.

We wasted our precious time. Fear, worry, doubt, and unbelief are time stealers. These habits are the result of not believing God is who he says he is and can do what he says he can do. Stop wasting your time—just believe. While you're waiting for your promise, do something nice for someone else.

I think Solomon had the best attitude about time when he wrote,

> There is a time for everything, and a season for every activity under heaven: a time to be born and a time to die, a time to plant and a time to uproot, a time to kill and a time to heal, a time to tear down and a time to build, a time to weep and a time to laugh, a time to mourn and a time to dance, a time to scatter stones and a time to gather them, a time to embrace and a time to refrain, a time to search and a time to give up, a time to keep and a time to throw away, a time to tear and a time to mend, a time to be silent and a time to speak, a time to love and a time to hate, a time for war and a time for peace. (Eccl. 3:1-8)

There is a time for everything. God has given us enough time for all he has for us to do. Every day is full and well balanced. We should rejoice and be glad in it.

We may misuse it or abuse it but the misconception of not having enough time is a lie from the devil. If we believe him, we will never start or finish anything.

Just like God, the devil has a destiny in mind for us, too. His desire is for us to get stuck—paralyzed in unbelief. Fear kills motivation, making us unproductive. Worry depresses us, keeping us overwhelmed and miserable. Ultimately, the devil wants us to self-destruct. That's why he will set us up to lose.

Listen! God has set us up to win by setting "eternity in the hearts of men" (Eccl. 3:11). God wants us to think like he thinks. He wants us to know without a doubt what he has prepared for us.

If you meditate on this Scripture long enough, you will take on an eternity mind-set. It will become as real to you as the air you breathe. In the world of eternity, you stop worrying about not having enough time. Your days on earth become perfectly blessed, as you bring heaven to earth. No longer is time a concern because time is endless.

When my oldest son, Jason, was married, it was the longest day of my life. Let me add that it was also one of the most perfect days. When my children were infants, I started praying for their mates. I knew their future would become who they married. I prayed and prayed and prayed some more.

I know God heard me the first time, but I needed to build up my own faith. Anyway, I prayed a very long time for Jason because he was thirty when Amanda came into his life. She was perfect for him and for our family.

I woke up that morning with a smile on my face that never left. I thought, "This is going to be a wonderful day. I want to take it all in; I will not miss a thing." I had waited so long for this dream to come true.

As the day played forward, I felt like everything moved in slow motion. Time was on my side. I wasn't rushed. I was able to enjoy the moment and lock into my memory all the events of the day. I connected with everyone and I still remember conversations I had with family and friends.

> *Time is forever.*
>
>

I didn't miss anything. I can still hear the music that played as I danced with my son. The entire wedding day was captured in my heart forever and I will never forget it. Lying in bed that night I thought, "God, you gave me a perfect day."

Why am I telling you this? Because I want you to have perfect days in your life. I want you to experience what God has set up for you. I want you to enjoy your life on this earth to the max.

It was the longest day of my life because I decided it would be. I didn't let the time stealers invade my world. I was determined to enjoy the blessing of every moment. I had set my heart to live in my setup.

An eternity mind-set releases you to live each day to its fullest. You are connected to the power of eternal life that moves you into your setup.

You are caught up into the realm of the Spirit, where his Spirit guides everything you do. In this realm, time doesn't matter. God has promised that goodness and love will follow you all the days of your life. You are not limited by the boundary of time. Time is forever.

CHAPTER FOUR

Divine Intervention

God's handprint upon your life leaves the marking of miracles. His divine intervention is continually setting you up to walk out his perfect order for your life. God is as near to you as your own heartbeat. As your heavenly Father, it is his pleasure to assist you in your everyday walk of life.

God has prophetically pronounced your future and strategically set himself up to be a vital part of making it happen. His inescapable presence is always there to help you do the impossible. God intervenes sometimes when we least expect it to reveal his covenant of unfailing love and his divine nature.

Most of us acknowledge his intervention when we're miraculously saved from disaster. So it was with Michael Lienau. Michael joined a film crew to capture the first ground-level shots of Mount St. Helens's volcanic eruption.

> *God has prophetically pronounced your future and strategically set himself up to be a vital part of making it happen.*

You've Been Set Up

Ready with his camera, he jumped out of a helicopter into what was called "ground zero," a wasteland of flattened timbers that looked like a nuclear holocaust.

Common sense told him not to go but the young twenty-year-old filmmaker ignored the warning. He was sure that this film would be his big breakthrough to stardom, the moment he had been waiting for. But it would soon deteriorate into a living nightmare.

The three-hour-thrill shoot became a three-day struggle for survival. His compass was useless by magnetism in the hot fresh ash, and the altered terrain and slopes caused by the eruption made the contour maps meaningless. The struggle to walk out of the devastation now became a death march as he fought fatigue, hunger, and hopelessness.

At two o'clock in the morning, Mount St. Helens erupted for the second time. The ground shook. The blast rocketed over their heads causing hot ash to pour down on them, making it hard to breathe. In a moment of desperation, Michael prayed, "God, help me breathe." All at once it started to rain, clearing the air so he could breathe.

Michael had been raised in a Christian home but hadn't considered his own personal relationship with Christ. Now, terrified and facing death, he cried out to God for help. "Make yourself real to me, God."

He reached in his pocket and pulled out a minisized Bible his father had given to him. Blindly flipping through the pages, he opened to "in all these things we are more than conquerors through him who loved us. For I am convinced that neither death nor life, neither angels nor demons, neither the present nor the future, nor any powers, neither height nor depth, nor anything else in all creation, will be able to separate us from the love of God that is in Christ Jesus our Lord" (Rom. 8:37-40).

From that moment on, Michael was filled with peace. He felt the presence of the Lord, as if God was walking alongside of him. He knew that whether he lived or died, he would be OK.

Divine Intervention

Two days later, still struggling to survive, he felt his body slipping into hypothermia. All he wanted to do was fall asleep and wake up from this horrible nightmare. While sleeping, he experienced a spiritual vision. He vividly saw the crucifixion and resurrection of Christ. Then he heard a song by George Clinton that grew louder and louder, "He's alive and I'm forgiven, Heaven's gates are open wide."

When Michael awoke, he saw an image of Christ limping, crawling, and carrying a broken tree on his back. The image of what Christ had suffered for him brought a surge of energy to his body. He got up and started walking. For once the fog had cleared and he could see two faint lights flashing on top of two military rescue helicopters. They were moving away from him, heading down the valley back to their base.

Michael fell down on his hands and knees and prayed, "Lord, I'm twenty years old and I will dedicate the rest of my life serving you if you get [me] out of this mess." Moments later, he saw the blades of a helicopter rise over the hill and fly down to his location. He was saved.

Today, Michael and his wife, Shari, and their children live in Washington State where they are involved in the production of films that glorify the name of the Lord. He kept his promise to the Lord and has had the opportunity to share his story to audiences all over the world.[1]

God became real to Michael, which changed his life forever. He was on a path that could have brought death but God had a destiny for him to fulfill. God intervened in Michael's tragedy to rescue him, to set him in place to accomplish what God had planned for him to do. "Many are the plans in a man's heart, but it is the Lord's purpose that prevails" (Prov. 19:21).

> *God will not force you to do it but he is the force in you to make it happen.*
>
>

You've Been Set Up

You, also, have been chosen by God and have a predestined plan to carry out his will. God will not force you to do it but he is the force in you to make it happen.

Your life and destiny have great significance to the world. You have been called, by his goodness, for a specific purpose that no one else could do as well as you. Furthermore, he has equipped you with everything you need to do it. You possess his divine nature to do the impossible. Expect his imminent supernatural involvement in your life. Impossibilities become realities when you are linked up with God through divine birth.

When my daughter-in-law, Juliane, moved back to Arizona after attending school in California, she went out looking for a job. A position in her field of artistry was hard to find, so for the short term she decided to apply for a position that had just opened at our church.

During the interview, Juliane found out that the job was a secretarial position which she felt did not fit her personality or skills. Juliane was an artist and her passion was in creating something new every day, not having the same routine day after day. The thought of answering phones, typing, and doing any type of math was out of the question.

Realizing she did not want the job, Juliane thought, "I'll make sure they know I am not qualified so I won't be hired."

"How fast do you type?"

"I don't type."

"Are you familiar with computers?"

"No, I don't even have a computer!"

"Have you ever answered phones?"

"Never!"

"Do you have any background in accounting?"

"Absolutely not!"

After a short pause and a glance at her resume, they looked up at her and to her amazement, said, "OK, you're hired. You'll start on Monday."

Divine Intervention

Over the years, we have had more laughs about that interview! Juliane could not escape the plan of God for her life. Today, she has been working happily for eight years, faithfully serving and following the plan of God for her life.

God did not leave her in a position that didn't utilize her gifts or passions. On the contrary, she has learned and developed more skills that have enhanced her goals and equipped her for greater success in her destiny. God opened doors for her to do things that she never dreamed she would be doing.

What looked like a mundane, short-term job turned out to be the perfect way for God to get Juliane where she needed to be. God's intervention during the interview made them want to hire her no matter what she said. God gave her favor.

"We know that in all things God works for the good of those who love him…If God is for us, who can be against us?" (Rom. 8:28, 31).

The truth is, God is constantly interfering in your business. He is a father that is involved with his children. He knows what's best for you. He knows the plans he has for us and is able to communicate those plans to us in extraordinary ways.

God is speaking to his children all the time. Through nature, dreams, visions, the voice of a child, the encouragement of a true friend, and in Juliane's case, her boss. He is eagerly waiting for you to hear and engage with him.

Most often his intervention is taken for granted or mistaken as a coincidence. "Good luck" is often tagged on to the person who is being blessed, instead of recognizing that the help really came from heaven. Others have

> *The truth is, God is constantly interfering in your business.*

discovered that God intervened and led them so powerfully that their lives were undeniably transformed and redirected; all because heaven invaded their world.

Because of his amazing grace and unconditional love, we have all received favors, help, approval, and many benefits we haven't deserved. God daily compliments us with goodness. He is in the business of making sure his children are blessed, happy, satisfied, and doing his will.

Consider this: Every story in the Bible was written to increase our understanding of the nature of God and increase our faith to believe beyond our natural senses. Likewise, every single person written about in the Bible had a personal encounter with God that changed their life dramatically.

Because of God's intervention, the ordinary people in the Bible became heroes. Deborah, a housewife, became a judge. Moses, a stutterer, became a deliverer. David, a shepherd boy, became a king. Joseph, a prisoner, became a prime minister. Esther, an orphan, became a queen. John the Baptist, a vagabond, became the forerunner of Jesus. Mary, an unknown virgin, gave birth to the Son of God. Paul, a self-righteous persecutor, became the greatest missionary in history and the author of two-thirds of the New Testament.

> *Allow your Maker to assist you in becoming the champion you want to be.*
>
>

There's a hero in you, too. Allow your Maker to assist you in becoming the champion you want to be. You cannot think it unusual for God to interact in your daily life. He is your heavenly Father who holds you in the palm of his hand. He is the one who will never leave you or forsake you. God seeks to reveal himself to you whether you seek him or not. You've been set up to meet him on the road of your life.

Stop ignoring his presence. Open up your heart to receive his guidance. He is the

Divine Intervention

only one that can get you where you need to be. You will never get lost following his directions. He will take you down the road less traveled and you will see and do things you never thought possible.

Maybe you feel like your life is going nowhere right now. Do you feel stuck in a rut? You may have made some bad decisions and now you're paying the price. Maybe you don't feel worthy to have God involved in your life. Or you just can't believe that God has a plan and future for you.

All that negative thinking will keep you bound, paralyzed, and useless. You may as well go down to your city jail, handcuff yourself, live behind those prison doors, and throw away the keys.

That's called being a fool. The heart of a fool blurts out folly because he is full of stinking thinking.

You can look back over your life and ask God, "Where have you been?" Or better yet, you should look back and say, "Thank God I'm here today. Lord, you have spared my life and placed me in position to receive favor and blessing." The fact that you wake up every morning is a gift from God.

Taking one small step can pull you out of your misery. One single word can light up your heart with hope. One person is waiting for you to call on his name. Just say, "Jesus, be real to me. I need you. Your love has covered every right and every wrong thing in my life. I'm ready for you to turn me in your direction. Tune me into your divine intervention in my life."

Make it a habit to dig up the good things from your past. Pinpoint the times in your life when you were truly happy. Remember the times when you were amazed, thrilled, or astonished. God should be credited and thanked because he is the author of everything good in this world.

As you look back, remember people that made you feel good about yourself and encouraged you in your endeavors. Realize that God was the source of those blessings. Thank him. Be grateful. When you appreciate and meditate on his goodness in your past, it gives you hope for your future.

When I get down in the dumps and things aren't happening as fast as I think they should, I close my eyes; for some reason, doing that helps me block out my circumstances. Then I remember all the amazing things God has done for me, from stretching my gas tank to saving my children in major car accidents. I remind myself of his intervention in my life, the blessings that only God could be responsible for.

I remember how I stared for hours through the window of the nursery after I gave birth to our first child. Kelli was the most beautiful baby ever born. Well, just until I had my four sons.

As a newly pregnant woman, I was in awe of the whole marvel of pregnancy and birth. I cherished every moment, increasingly aware of the wonder that was growing inside of me. As God was perfectly hand making Kelli's every feature, he was giving me a chance to assist him with a miracle.

I felt a glimpse of his love for me by the feelings I had for her.

The love I felt for her was all-encompassing, a love I had never felt before. Nothing could ever separate me from her. This love held my full attention. All I thought about was how I would care for her and give her the best life possible. I couldn't wait to be her mom. I birthed her and she was mine!

Stop now and think about a blessing in your life that you know God was responsible for. Dream about it for a few minutes. Live it all over again. Feel what you felt at that time—those good emotions are from God, too. Allow yourself to feel good. God is restoring your soul right now. Give him this moment. Set the book down and let God intervene.

CHAPTER FIVE

What You See Is What You Get

We are told never to cross a bridge till we come to it,
but this world is owned by men who have "crossed bridges"
in their imagination far ahead of the crowd.
—Speakers Library

Faith is seeing your dream come true before it happens. With the eye of imagination, you form a mental picture of something that is not present to your natural senses. You create in your mind what you desire to have in the physical realm. When your heart discerns as truth what you created in your mind, the Bible calls that faith.

Without faith, it's impossible to please God. Faith is the substance of things hoped for and the evidence of things not seen, according to Hebrews 11:1. Your God-given imagination gives substance to what you believe to have and is God's way of making your dreams come true. The Word gives us permission to dream and while we're at it, to dream big.

> *Faith is seeing your dream come true before it happens.*
>
>

When I was in high school, I spent a lot of time daydreaming in class. I have to admit, I wasn't into the textbooks. I had a desire to learn but was bored with the subjects and most of my teachers.

I was able to get good grades without really paying attention in class, so I chose to live in my world of make-believe, where everything was beautiful. Hours would fly by, while in my mind, I was creating my weekend, my next date, and the dreams of my future.

I didn't realize that I was actually planning success into my life. The power of the imagination was not yet a revelation to me. But today, as I look back, I find that all my dreams came true. To my astonishment, what I envisioned actually happened.

When you spend time dreaming, you paint a picture in your mind of what you want. Your wants or desires reveal the secret longings of your heart. Now you are getting in touch with what God desires for you to have because he is the one who put those dreams in your heart to begin with.

> *Dreaming puts you in touch with God.*
>
>

Dreaming puts you in touch with God. Your imaginings bypass your conscious mind which tells you what you can or can't have, and move you into the realm of faith where all things are possible. The longer you stay in faith, the more apt you are to obtain the desire you believe for.

You are actually programming your subconscious mind. The subconscious mind believes whatever you tell it to, then it automatically moves you toward your goal. When you know what you want, you know what to look for. You are attracted to the things you desire. Unless you change your mind or stray from your goal, you will eventually obtain it.

This concept works every time. Faith works every time. For centuries, men have written books explaining the power of thoughts and the amazing part of our brain called the sub-conscious. But the origins of these truths are found in the Word of God. God made the brain and he tells us how to use it for our good.

The secrets of the kingdom of God are all in the Book. Today, godly men and women, doctors, success motivators, and business speakers all over the world teach these godly principles and write them in their books. But the origin of this infinite knowledge is God.

Understand the power of dreaming and seeing your future through God's eyes. To live in your setup, you must long to see what God has planned for your life. If you ask him, he will show you. The true-you will be revealed little by little.

When you desire the will of God for your life, he will be faithful to lead you right into it. Believe he can do what he says he can do. Your dreams are never too big for God. Make a demand on yourself to get in touch with the Spirit of God within you and choose to dream with him.

In 2008, four relatives—my niece, daughter-in-law, sister-in-law, and I—started a business called Nanny Caddy. As quoted in the February 2009 *Pregnancy & Newborn* national magazine: "One day I was with my aunt Mary June, my close friend Juliane and my mom when out of the blue my aunt said, 'You know I just really feel like we are to invent something.' I was shocked because I hadn't mentioned my idea to anyone but my immediate family. So I said, 'I have just the thing.' And told them about this vending machine that would stock diapers, wipes, bottles, pacifiers and more. They loved it, and our team for Nanny Caddy was formed that day!"

My niece Celena had been dreaming about her idea for almost two years. When it's a God idea, not just a good idea, you just can't let it go. It keeps coming up in your mind over and over again, combined with joy and excitement.

When God gives you a dream, he has already set you up to make it happen. To walk into your setup, you must stay in tune with God. He will direct your footsteps right to the people and other resources you need to make it happen. God is more excited than you to see it happen because it was birthed in his heart first.

The four of us women, with our husbands, created Nanny Caddy. Each person committed themselves to work in a specific area. Every skill needed was found within the group. We had been set up for success.

Within four months, we had our first vending machine fashionably decorated and ready to go. Our first customer proved to be the closest mall. Landing our first location was a piece of cake. The person in charge of mall operations fell in love with the concept and the chic design of the machine. We had such favor with her, she discounted the rent for our space in the mall and bent over backwards to set our machine in the perfect spot.

Nanny Caddy drew the attention of every mom and dad. Letters started to come in to the Web site thanking us for such a great service. At the same time, we also started getting attention from the media. The local TV station gave us a spot on their evening news. A month later, two local magazines wrote articles about Nanny Caddy.

> *We are faithful to do our part and he is faithful to do more than we can ever dream.*
>
>

Then when *Pregnancy & Newborn Magazine* featured Nanny Caddy just ten months running, that launched us into a whole new world and a much bigger vision. Calls are continually coming in and now we are expanding throughout the country.

To God be all the glory. We are faithful to do our part and he is faithful to do more than we can ever dream. Since he set us up to be successful, we expect to walk right into success; everything our hands touch will prosper. God opens doors that people can't open.

What You See Is What You Get

God can work with a vision. He's that one that causes you to dream according to his purposes. Turn it all over to him and watch your vision become a reality. When your dream and his match up, the sky will be the limit and you will be flooded with all the resources you could ever need.

Get a glimpse of what God has for you. Ask to see into the realm of the Spirit where God created all things in the first place. As a Christian, this realm should be real and normal for you. The more time you spend meditating on the Word of God, the more acquainted you will be with the realm of his Spirit.

It's not spooky or scary. Neither is it weird. You are a spirit being. It's where you came from and where you're going. You may as well get familiar with it now and enjoy the benefits of life blessed by the Spirit.

More than anything, God wants you to get the vision that he has for your life. Once you get a glimpse of what he has set you up to accomplish and enjoy in this life, you will have the power to make it happen.

One afternoon, I was taking a walk through my neighborhood and I was moved to pray for my neighbors. I wondered how many of them really knew God and the joy of living the Christian life. I was feeling very blessed that day just knowing how much my Lord had done for me.

Suddenly, this thought passed through my mind: "You should have a Bible study in your home and invite all the women in your neighborhood." I just kept walking and wondering where that thought came from.

Then again: "You should start praying about having a Bible study in your home and invite all the women in your neighborhood." I thought, "Oh! I can do that!" Praying is what I did best—I felt fully capable of that part of the idea.

So I did. Every time I walked through my neighborhood, I prayed for all my neighbors to know God and serve him with all of their hearts and to experience all the blessings of being a Christian. "And, Lord, prepare me to have a Bible study in my home," I would add.

We moved out of that neighborhood and I never had a Bible study in my home. But in my next neighborhood, I continued to pray for my old neighborhood and added the new one to all the prayers.

Almost every morning, my husband and I would walk and pray. I would always add my prayers for the neighbors, along with the usual, "Lord, prepare me to have a Bible study in my home."

Five years went by, and although I never felt led to have a Bible study, I kept praying. Then we moved to another neighborhood. And yes, I started to pray for that neighborhood, too. But now when I prayed, I desired to start a Bible study right away.

Consequently, I started to ask God to show me how. I didn't know anybody, and why would they come if they didn't know me? Then one morning, I ran into a girlfriend who had lived in the very first neighborhood. Lo and behold, she invited me to a Bible study that was three doors down from my new house. I was pleasantly surprised!

I attended their next meeting, comprising a small group of about six ladies. They were ending their Bible study for the summer months and the lady who was hosting it in her home was moving out of town.

When I left her home that afternoon, God spoke to my heart, "Now is the time for the Bible study in your home." I was so excited! Finally, after twelve years, God released me to undertake the vision he had placed in my heart.

That fall, I invited seventy-five women in our new neighborhood to a brunch in my home. There I explained my intention to have a Bible study every week and I invited them all. I showed them the materials we would be studying and had books available for them to buy that day. It was to start the very next week.

The following week, twenty hungry women showed up in my family room. Women hungry for God, for the Word, and for meaningful relationships. I was amazed how the Holy Spirit led us each week in the study

What You See Is What You Get

of the Word and prayer. We were very blessed with the presence of the Lord and he met every need. Rumor spread throughout the neighborhood that we had something good going on.

The next year, I invited one hundred women for brunch in my home. As a result, God multiplied our little Bible study group to forty-eight women. I have been astonished by how God is moving in these women's lives. Each can share their own testimony of being touched, inspired, healed, delivered, and loved. We have witnessed many miracles and answers to prayer. And it all started with a passing thought that planted a vision in my heart.

"Where there is no vision, the people perish" (Prov. 29:18 KJV). If you ask people, "Why do you exist?" most cannot tell you. They can't explain their purpose in the world. They have no vision for their lives.

Get in touch with the vision God has put inside of you. Think about your deepest desires. Let yourself dream about who God created you to be. Write down your thoughts. Think of yourself with no limitations.

Think back over your life. When were you the happiest? What were you doing? What do you wish you could do? What are your persistent thoughts about?

Vision persists. Your purpose is that undeniable urge inside of you that surfaces every once in a while.

Vision persists.

Capture a meaning for your life, a clear meaning for your existence. You don't have to know the big picture to get started. Just be faithful with what you see right now. As you follow your dream, the vision will expand and become clearer.

Vision keeps you moving forward. Dreams draw out of you what God has put inside of you when he created you. What he put inside of you, he enabled you to do.

Vision needs to be specific and focused on your strongest talents. Don't try to do someone else's dream or something you know nothing about. God's assignment for you emphasizes your greatest assets. You have everything within you to fulfill the dream.

> *God's assignment for you emphasizes your greatest assets.*
>
>

The problem is that most people have no vision beyond their current circumstance. Without a vision of the future, life loses its meaning. Vision is the key to life because where there's a dream, there's hope, and where there's hope, there's faith. Faith brings the unseen into the present.

God has placed in every human being a unique vision and call that is designed to give purpose and meaning to life. You are an original, not a knockoff of someone else. Inside of you is someone different than anyone else. When you find that person, you will find fulfillment. Fulfillment is complete realization of who you are supposed to be.

> *You are an original, not a knockoff of someone else.*
>
>

CHAPTER SIX

Do You Have a Heart Condition?

Are you sitting on top of the fence trying to figure out what side you want to be on? Do you feel like you're on a teeter-totter—up, down, up, down?

What do you believe for? *Really.* Stop and ask yourself, "What do I believe in my heart about my life? What am I all about? Where am I headed?"

In other words, where is your faith? What do you have faith in concerning your life? You have faith for something. It could be for positive, exciting, and good things. Or you may be in faith for a life that is far below your potential and the destiny God has for you.

Humble yourself to take an honest look inside your heart to see what's in there. Step aside and take a look at your life as if you were standing in someone else's shoes. What do you see?

Do you see someone who is happy and excited about life, waking up every morning with a smile on their face? Do you see yourself making strides towards your dreams, accomplishing your goals and expecting great things to happen every day?

Are you enjoying meaningful relationships with your family and friends? Are you believing for God's best in your life or settling for less?

You've Been Set Up

What is the condition of your heart? Is it strong, full of faith, joy, and peace? Is your heart beating to the sound of life, following the voice of wisdom?

King David was a man after God's own heart. More than anything else, he wanted to please God and be faithful to do his will. David knew the only way he could do that was to keep his heart pure.

We read in the Psalms how David continually poured his heart out to God. These are his words: "May the words of my mouth and the meditation of my heart be pleasing in your sight, O Lord, my Rock and my Redeemer" (Ps. 19:14).

King David made many mistakes in his life, yet the Bible states that his heart was right before God; it was pure and pleasing in God's sight. Why? David realized that only God could change his heart.

David was willing to admit to himself that he had weaknesses that kept him from doing what was right. And he knew that only God had the power to save him from himself. Only God could purify his heart and set him free from the things that dragged him down and tripped him up. To get into the setup for his life, he must keep his heart pure.

David again expresses his heart by saying, "I seek you with all my heart; do not let me stray from your commands. I have hidden your word in my heart that I might not sin against you...My soul is consumed with longing for your law at all times...Turn my eyes away from worthless things; preserve my life according to your word" (Ps. 119:10-11, 20, 37).

David laid his heart out before the Lord and said, "Change me!" He didn't hide his faults in self-denial. He didn't make excuses or pretend his weaknesses didn't exist. He willingly opened up his heart and cried out to God, "Do surgery! Set me free!"

I would like to tell you that I had the ideal childhood and grew up in a home of love, acceptance, joy, and laughter. Unfortunately, that's not the way it was. Like many of you, my childhood memories were full of disappointments, anger, and abuse. Our dysfunctional family survived the outburst and abuse of a very angry father. My dad was a child in a grown-up's body that always had to have his own way, and most definitely, the last word.

Living a rag-to-riches story, his fame led him into the world of all kinds of addictions, which led our family into heartbreak after heartbreak. He was the absent father, always out there doing his own thing, leaving his family behind. When he did come home, you never knew which personality would be shining through—the good, the bad, or the ugly.

My dad just didn't know how to do family. He never realized the gift that God had given him. He wasn't there to give fatherly advice, teach you how to ride a bike, or give a kiss good night. During my three years of cheerleading, he never once saw me cheer. On parents' night my senior year, I stood alone with my mom. I need not say any more.

Because I had such a loving and caring mother, I didn't realize how much his lack of love and attention affected my life. She had taken on the role of mom *and* dad, so I was fine. At least I thought I was.

When we moved to Arizona, I never missed my dad. The only time I really thought to call him was Father's Day. Picking out a card seemed hypocritical. Reading them made me feel sick inside, realizing what I never experienced. But I went through the motions, ignoring the emotions. I was supposed to do the right thing. The bitterness and hatred for my dad was hidden deeply away.

Surprisingly, one Christmas he sent cards to my children (his grandchildren). Good ole Grandpa had the wrong names on the envelopes. That hit me like a bolt of lightning. "What is wrong with him!" I scoffed. "He doesn't even know his grandchildren's names?" What came out of my mouth next is unprintable. To say the least, I totally lost it. For the next hour, I totally crucified my loser of a father, bringing up to the surface one hurt after another.

I remember that night, lying in bed and crying myself to sleep. Through my tears, I asked God to take all the hatred and bitterness out of my heart. I was fully aware that God's command was to honor my father and my mother no matter what. And that command came with a promise. The promise to live a long and prosperous life.

Sure, I wanted the good life, but most of all I wanted to please God. I wanted to love my father unconditionally.

Not long after that, we planned a family trip back to Ohio. I called my dad ahead of time, which I had never done before, and asked him if I could spend the night in his home (my mother and he were divorced and he was remarried).

I had made a decision in my heart to forgive him. I made myself let go of all the hurt and every bad memory that I had in my heart. I asked God to heal the wounds of the past and give me his compassion towards my dad. I asked for a new beginning, a new love for him that was unconditional. And on that overnight stay, for the first time, I was able to say, "I love you, Dad!" and sincerely mean it.

That was two years before my father died. At his bedside, just hours before his death, we prayed together the prayer of salvation. With hardly any breath left, he whispered the prayer with tears running down his cheeks.

I knew at that moment that no matter how he had lived his life, he was now on his way to heaven. God forgave him in an instant and would remember his sins no more. I was so thankful that I had forgiven him too. Someday I will be with him in heaven and we will continue our new relationship.

Challenges we face in life have a way of bringing out the good and the bad in us. The way we handle trials reveals the condition of our hearts.

I was like a pressure cooker whose lid had popped off from all the steam of anger in my heart. When the lid came off, the anger, resentment, and hatred were exposed. I realized that those emotions were like cancer in my heart. Eventually, they would kill me.

Working through long-lived emotions takes courage. It's like facing a giant Dracula. You don't want to move towards it; you're afraid it might swallow you up.

Do You Have a Heart Condition?

You have to know that God is with you. He holds your right hand and says, "Fear not." The Lord is close to the brokenhearted and saves those who are crushed in spirit. He heals the brokenhearted and binds up their wounds.

Wounds need healing. You can't be productive in your setup until you get your heart condition healed. You won't be able to work at your maximum potential until your heart is strong and healthy.

One of the most dangerous conditions of the heart is a hardened heart. That's a case of losing your sensitivity towards the voice of God, where the only voice you want to hear is your own.

Sometimes this condition comes as a result of not getting your own way; God has let you down, your dream or promise didn't happen when and how you thought it should, and now you're mad and turn away from God.

Trials do have a way of making us weary and weighing us down. Life is not fair and some people seem to go through more hard times than others. Comparing your war wounds to someone else's and thinking you got the short end of the stick is the worst thing you can do. You may as well dig a slimy pit and jump in. You'll get yourself stuck in self-pity and cause your heart to become hardened.

When the Israelites were wandering around in the desert for forty years, their hearts became hardened with unbelief. What should have been an eleven-day trip took forty years. Why? They wouldn't listen to God.

They were bent on believing their circumstances instead of trusting God to lead them into the Promised Land. They were stubborn, self-directed, and determined to do it their own way. That's why they stayed in the desert and died in the desert.

Death is the result of a sinful, unbelieving heart. Death to your setup, death to the victory you could have in life. Ultimately, death to your relationship with God. We are warned time and time again in the Word of God that if we allow foolishness to rule in our hearts, causing them to become hardened, sin will consume our lives.

Today if you hear his voice, do not harden your heart. God's way is always the best way. He wants to move those hindrances out of your life so you can see your setup and know that he's in charge. He still sits on the throne, ready and willing to act on your behalf.

He has the power to bring all things in your life in line with his Word. Listen up! Settle down and submit to his will. Turn your voice down; better yet, turn it off so you can hear his leading. It's beyond good—it's spectacular!

Another popular heart condition is an unforgiving heart. Being unwilling to forgive someone will cut off your set-up support system. It's like unplugging your refrigerator in Phoenix and thinking the food won't spoil. Unforgiveness rots the bones and sucks the life right out of you. It makes you sick and tired, worn out. It's the worst poison of all.

Unless you're a hermit, every day offers opportunities to be upset or mad at someone. The truth is, whether you're at work, school, home, or at the grocery store, someone can tick you off.

The devil works overtime to get us upset. He is the accuser: "They treated you unfairly, they spread lies about you, you don't deserve to be treated like that after all you have done for them!"

> *Payback mentality is unforgiveness.*
>
>

Someone may have hurt you with his or her words. Or you didn't get invited to the party. Or someone is taking advantage of you. Maybe you were abused, divorced, abandoned. Whatever the case may be, you feel like you have the right to be mad.

Now you want to get back at them, making them pay for hurting you. You scheme, you plan; you're not going to let them hurt you again. You think, "I'll show them. They'll be sorry they ever messed with me."

What's happening? Where are you going? Human nature wants to pay back; the offender needs to be punished appropriately and feel the pain.

Do You Have a Heart Condition?

These kinds of feelings and thinking keep the fire going. Payback mentality is unforgiveness. You're been putting another log on the fire and now you've got a bonfire going. It's getting hotter and hotter and harder to put out. What will be left when the fire burns out?

If you keep it going, how many other people will be damaged by the smoke? Realize that when you hold unforgiveness in your heart, it's not just about you and the other person involved. It has an effect on every person in your inner circle.

Payback may feel good at the moment, but afterwards, you become the biggest loser of all. If you cannot forgive others, the Bible tells us that God cannot forgive you. If you sow unforgiveness, you reap unforgiveness. It's just not worth it. Give it up! Let go of those thoughts and feelings. Demand your heart to be purged of that trash.

Instead, decide to love. Love covers over a multitude of sins. Love never fails.

Many years ago, someone really hated me. They had no problem letting everyone know they hated me. They even went as far as telling others that they hated my entire family. This person spread lies about me, resulting in some of my closest friends turning their backs on me. It was a very dark time in my life.

I continually prayed and asked God what I had done to cause that person to feel this way. Every time, he would answer me, "Keep your heart pure! Love never fails!" And I would respond, "OK, Lord, I will do that and trust that you are going to turn this situation around."

One day I heard that they had undergone surgery. I called and ordered flowers to be sent to their home. I never heard back, but it was my way of letting them know that I held nothing against them, even though that person hated my family and me.

A few years went by, and then I heard that the person had moved away. God had removed them from my life. I no longer had to deal with feeling

> *Decide what you are not going to let into your heart before it comes your way.*
>
>

rejection every time I was around them. After that person was out of the picture and the truth was revealed, my destroyed relationships were healed.

Love never fails! There is only one debt that we have in this life and that is the debt to love others. Sincere love springs out of a pure heart. According to Proverbs 4:23, you have to guard your heart with all diligence, for out of it flows the issues of life. Put your guard up! Decide what you are not going to let into your heart *before* it comes your way.

Behave proactively and set your standards high. You can't let your heart be polluted by other people's choices. You can't let your heart be contaminated by the world and its ways.

Once you set your standards, don't compromise. So many times I wanted to lash back, build my own team, and jump in the game of maliciousness. Every time I had this notion, I would have to say out loud, "No! I won't do that. I am a Christian. Help me, Jesus! Give me the strength I need right now to say no to ungodliness. I desire to live free of unforgiveness and any other heart condition."

One of God's promises to us is that he will make even our enemies to be at peace with us. If you choose to do it God's way, he can turn the worst-case scenario into a blessing. If the other person wills to continue in their sin, he will remove them from your life. When God's on your side, no weapon formed against you shall prosper, promises Isaiah 54:17.

He rewards those who diligently seek him and do his will.

CHAPTER SEVEN
Life Isn't Fair but God Is

He conquers who endures.
—*Persius*

Life isn't fair, so get over it. Everyone will encounter a few bumps in the road. When you get serious about stepping up into your setup, all hell is going to break loose.

The enemy will throw his best shots at you to slow you down and get you off course. He doesn't want you to win in life and bring glory to God. You must be alert and ready to fight the good fight of faith like a hero instead of a victim.

"The greatest test of courage on earth is to bear defeat without losing heart," said orator Robert G. Ingersoll.

Phil Killey, a United States three-star general, was diagnosed with cancer in both kidneys. It was a shocking blow to a person who had spent his entire life in the air force as a fighter pilot and who was in tip-top physical shape.

Trained to never show fear, Phil had been a fighter pilot in the Vietnam War and had also flown numerous reconnaissance missions in other conflicts for our country.

You've Been Set Up

As soon as Phil heard the devastating report, he immediately had to fight in a different kind of war—the war against fear, the war against hopelessness in never fulfilling his destiny, and the war against death.

Along with the diagnosis of kidney cancer, the doctor also informed Phil and his wife of a suspected genetic disease called Von Hippel-Lindau, which could have been the reason for the kidney cancer. If tests proved this to be true, cancer would eventually show up in all his vital organs.

Immediately, Phil went through two major surgeries to remove his kidneys and through the long and difficult process of dialysis.

In his darkest hour, Phil could have easily become bitter. He could have easily said, "God, this is not fair. Why did this happen to me? I have laid down my life for my country and my fellow man and now you allow something like this to happen to me?" In short, he could have played the victim.

But self-pity was not in Phil's blood. Phil was determined to fight that fight like a hero and win. He knew that for him to beat this beast, he would have to depend on his Savior like never before.

Phil and his wife ran to God. God surrounded them with an entourage of prayer warriors. Encouragement flooded in from all around the world. During the 2008 presidential election, Senator John McCain, a comrade fighter pilot, phoned Phil to say his prayers were with him.

Immediately upon hearing the news, over thirty friends were willing to sacrifice a kidney to give to Phil. The love of God through the hearts of others served as a sedative to all the pain he was going through.

Phil's attitude was set to endure with dignity and to win. Three days after his first surgery, he walked a mile to my house, rang the doorbell and said, "Just taking a walk in the neighborhood." I couldn't help but think, "Are you kidding me?"

Phil kept the smile on his face and his zest for life. He never gave in to the constant symptoms of pain or weariness. While on dialysis, he continued to engage in conference calls with military committee members in DC.

Phil and his wife, Ellen, constantly gave praise for the supernatural strength that God provided for them each day. They praised God for every moment of life and certainly every breakthrough on the road to healing.

Months later, Phil was diagnosed cancer free and did not have Von Hippel-Lindau disease. If all went well, in two years he would be a candidate for a kidney transplant. Again, Phil beat the odds. In just one and a half years, his doctors approved a transplant. Now, which one of the thirty brave volunteers was set up to be the donor?

During this time, God had been speaking to one special woman. Without delay, she called Phil.

"Hi Dad! Just wanted to tell you that God told me that I was to give you a kidney."

Robin, Phil's daughter-in-law, was so excited as she told him the news. "I will be coming to Phoenix for testing right away."

A few days later, she checked into the Mayo Clinic for a series of tests which all proved out that she was the perfect match. Two weeks later, side by side, Phil and Robin were rolled into the surgery room. Phil looked over to Robin and said, "Hey, you still have time to back out."

"No way, Dad, it is an honor to do this for you."

Today, Phil is completely healed and he gives all the glory to God. It wasn't an overnight miracle, but a process. A process of walking into the setup of miracles.

> *A process of walking into the setup of miracles.*
>
>

Phil was never a victim to his circumstances. He ignored them to follow the route of healing that God was walking him through.

You've Been Set Up

Life isn't fair! The Bible warns us in John 10:10 that the enemy comes to kill, steal, and destroy. Temptations, trials, and difficulties will come. How we handle them decides the outcome.

God has a divine purpose for every challenge that comes into your life. He also has a divine way out of the valley of the shadow of death. He sets you up to walk victoriously to the other side, much stronger and wiser. When you walk through the fire, you might get burned, but you won't come out smelling like smoke.

First Peter 4:12-13 admonishes, "Do not be surprised at the painful trial you are suffering, as though something strange were happening to you. But rejoice that you participate in the sufferings of Christ, so that you may be overjoyed when his glory is revealed."

Trials will come, tragedies will happen—but never from God. God cannot create trouble. Contrary to popular belief, God does not put troubles in your life to teach you a good lesson. That's ridiculous!

Would you strike your child with cancer to make them stronger? Would you throw your child into the fire to teach them a lesson? Of course not. That's ludicrous! You would stand in front of a train to save the life of your child.

Parents lay down their lives to give their children all the things they never had. Let's face it; there's no greater joy in life than blessing those you love.

Trouble comes from the enemy. Trouble comes by the bad decisions we make with our own free will. Troubles come because we live in an imperfect world, thanks to Adam and Eve! They were the beginning of trouble.

Mankind is subject to the evil in this world. The perfect world passed away when Adam and Eve sinned in the garden. They messed up the perfect setup. In this world, trials and tribulation are a part of life.

Everyone experiences hard times. Be prepared for tough times. As a believer, you have authority over the devil. Don't let him push you around. Greater is the One inside of you.

Life Isn't Fair but God Is

Jehovah, the almighty God, is on your side. He is your answer. He is your way out of your trouble. He is the help you need. He is the Comforter, the Healer, the Restorer.

He is whatever you need him to be. Run to him, lean on his wisdom. Give God a chance to meet you. You won't be disappointed.

Don't be a victim of the enemy. Rise above the challenges, accept the things you cannot change, and change the things you can. During those trials, God is working all things out according to his will. When the pressure is on, even though it's painful, God will use those trials to cleanse you, purify your heart, and make you a stronger person.

Several years ago, our granddaughter Megan died at birth. When Kelli was five month's pregnant, tests revealed that Megan had a genetic chromosome disease.

My daughter and her husband, Jason, decided to pray and believe for a miracle. They spoke the Word of God over Megan every day. They wouldn't come into agreement with what the tests said; they stood on the promises of God and what the Word said.

Kelli and Jason did all they knew to do, spiritually and naturally, to receive a miracle for their daughter Megan. The whole family fasted, prayed, and believed for the miracle through which Megan would be healed and whole.

Normally, babies with this disease are aborted before the sixth month of pregnancy. However, Kelli carried Megan almost full term which gave us all-the-more faith to believe she was healed.

At thirty-five weeks, Megan was born but she only lived for a few short minutes. Megan was taken up to heaven by an angel and placed into the hands of the Lord.

At that moment, looking into Kelli and Jason's eyes, I saw disappointment, pain, and confusion. We were all shocked, all wondering the same thing: "Why didn't we get our miracle?"

A huge mountain was facing my daughter and son-in-law. What would their reaction be? How would they handle this loss? Would they fall apart, be bitter, live depressed, and continually ask God why?

Kelli and Jason held each other with tears in their eyes and said good bye to Megan. Then they began to pray for strength and wisdom.

How could we explain this to our other three children? We believed God for a miracle but it didn't happen the way we wanted.

Kelli and Jason didn't ask why. They knew there are many trials in life that cannot be explained. They were determined to rise above the tragedy, not giving the devil any glory by allowing doubt, unbelief, failure, or depression to enter their hearts.

Ultimately, the devil wanted to destroy their faith and put fear in their hearts with his accusations: "Ha! Ha! You found out that God's Word doesn't work. You didn't get your miracle because you didn't have enough faith. Does God's Word really say it's his will for all to be healed? Give it up! Give in! You're done!"

The devil's lies had no power over them. They boldly proclaimed, "God is a good God all the time. We will love him and serve him for the rest of our lives. We don't need to know the why; we just need to know the Way."

Four years later, they had a baby boy named Logan. He has been the fulfillment of their restoration. Today, they are stronger in their faith and minister powerfully as pastors. Their joy is in helping others work through the disappointments and challenges of life.

Psalm 34:19 is a comforting promise to always have in mind when you are going through the hard times: "A righteous man may have many troubles, but the Lord delivers him from them all."

Hallelujah! Now that is the truth.

When the storm hits, rise above your circumstances. Take captive all the negative thoughts and emotions that try to overcome you. Take a stand to believe that God's in charge, knowing that he sits on the throne. He knows what you're going through and has set you up to find the answer. In his hands lies your victory.

Face the hard times with courage. Adjust your attitude of perseverance up a level. Instead of getting mad and becoming a victim to your circumstance, decide to fight the fight with integrity. Be the hero, not the victim.

> *Adjust your attitude of perseverance up a level.*
>
>

In James 1:2-4 we are taught the true value of trials: "Consider it pure joy, my brothers, whenever you face trials of many kinds, because you know that the testing of your faith develops perseverance. Perseverance must finish its work so that you may be mature and complete, not lacking anything."

Individuals who are spiritually mature have the ability to withstand the storm. They are people who laugh at the days to come. Their emotions are stable and their thoughts are positive. They move into their setup and on to greater victories.

As Admiral William Frederick Halsey Jr. put it, "There aren't any great men. There are just great challenges that ordinary men like you and me are forced by circumstances to meet."

CHAPTER EIGHT

Choices Are Simple So Don't Make Them Difficult

A hardworking female executive dies and meets St. Peter at the pearly gates, where he says, "You've shown an outstanding aptitude for making business decisions. Choose whether you will go to heaven or to hell."

"I don't know!" she flounders.

"Tell you what," St. Peter says. "You can have 24 hours in heaven and 24 hours in hell. Then you have to decide where to spend eternity."

"Okay then," she says. "I'll start with heaven since I'm here already."

She goes in the pearly gates and makes some acquaintances. They have a nice walk among beautiful gardens. They have a nice quiet lunch. They have a nice stroll along a pristine, white, sandy beach looking out on brilliant, blue ocean. At the end of the day she is shown to a nice room, and has a quiet meal on the balcony, looking out over the setting sun and the ocean. She marvels at the scenic beauty of heaven.

The next morning, St. Peter takes her to the fiery gates of hell and hands her off to Satan.

You've Been Set Up

Satan takes her to a power breakfast given in her honor. Then she is escorted to a tennis club where she is greeted by her old boss, some co-workers, and previous business acquaintances. She plays a few sets of tennis and catches up on the gossip. At lunchtime her old boss takes her to a gourmet restaurant and she has an excellent meal with vintage wine.

After lunch he takes her to an exclusive golf course and they play 18 holes of golf. She runs into other business acquaintances and catches up on news and gossip.

After golf, he drops her at a spa where she is pampered and spoiled by beauty and body treatments. When she is finished at the spa, an acquaintance takes her shopping at designer stores. She picks out a fabulous evening gown, and Satan himself takes her to a huge party with dancing, gourmet food, and famous people.

At the end of the evening, a stretch limo drops her off at a five-star hotel. As she soaks in the Jacuzzi tub, and sips the complimentary champagne, she ponders eternity.

The next morning, she meets St. Peter at the pearly gates.

"Well, have you made your decision?" he asks.

"I've decided on hell," she announces.

"So be it." St. Peter waves good-bye and she reappears before the fiery gates of hell.

Once inside she is teamed up with her old boss again, only this time everyone is wearing rags. They are filthy, diseased, malnourished, and living in a barren desert. They have to scrounge for food, water, clothing, even shade.

"What happened!?!" she exclaimed.

"Well," said her boss. "Yesterday you were a recruit. Today you are staff."

> *You live with your choices. Good or bad, your free will puts you in the driver's seat.*

Choices Are Simple So Don't Make Them Difficult

You live with your choices. Good or bad, your free will puts you in the driver's seat. Your hands are on the steering wheel of life. You choose the direction you want to go.

Your choices form your future. Just as the life you have today is a result of the choices you made yesterday, tomorrow will be the result of what you've chosen today.

God has given man the power to choose the life he desires to live. In his Word, he charges us to make right choices.

"This day I call heaven and earth as witnesses against you that I have set before you life and death, blessings and curses. Now choose life, so that you and your children may live" (Deut. 30:19).

To choose life is to choose the life he designed for you to live. Choose to be who you were created to be. What God asks of you is not too difficult or beyond your reach. You are free to be you, just by making the right choice.

Choices are simple, so don't make them difficult. There are only two ways to go. You can either choose life or death, right or wrong. Make it a habit of choosing life.

Your choices affect the lives of future generations. Choose life so that you will live a good, long life and your children will inherit the blessing of your good choices. If you choose well, they will love the Lord and serve him with all of their heart. That's a promise.

Making a right choice should be exciting. Yes, sometimes it's tough to get your flesh to agree to the best choice. The flesh is weak and every now and again you might want to give in and make the wrong choice. You know what I mean—chocolate always wins!

The truth is that the harder we are on ourselves, the easier life is going to be. To train your free will to always choose life is to conquer the flesh and its desires. Then you are truly free.

Novelist Ayn Rand stated, "That which you call your soul or spirit is your consciousness, and that which you call 'free will' is your mind's freedom to think or not, the only will you have, your only freedom, the choice that controls all the choices you make and determines your life and your character."

Maybe your parents were bad examples. Maybe you've been hanging with the wrong crowd that makes bad choices and you've been going along with them. Now you feel stuck.

You could be dealing with an addiction to alcohol or drugs and you feel powerless to stop. You've found a way to live with your weaknesses and settle for less than the blessed life.

You need to remember that every wrong choice has a consequence. Sooner or later, you will pay for the bad decision that you made. Down the road comes the fruit of decision because you reap what you sow. Every choice you make has an end result.

Stop and think about what you are forfeiting every time you make the wrong choice. How does your decision affect those around you?

What is the result of your decision to sleep in and be late for work? Who will that affect? What is the result of eating fried food and soda pop? What will that do to your body?

What is the result of having a one-night affair? What is the result of watching the game on Sunday, instead of going to church? If you would pause to think through your decisions, the result will keep you from making a lot of wrong choices that you will regret.

Unfortunately, we are familiar with some of the greatest actors who ever lived, yet who died young as a result of a bad decision. Comedy legend John Candy, who starred in *Uncle Buck* and *Planes, Trains & Automobiles* died of a heart attack at age forty-three. Judy Garland, the star of the *Wizard of Oz*, died of an accidental drug overdose when she was forty-seven.

Choices Are Simple So Don't Make Them Difficult

After fourteen hours of debate, Congress approved two articles of impeachment against President Clinton. A house resolution charged him with lying under oath to a federal grand jury and obstructing justice. Do you think he may have regretted the choices he made?

I hate regret. Yet, it has a way of making you not go down the same road. Once you've paid a high price for a big mistake, learn from it. Don't be a fool. The next time, listen to your conscience. Be smarter.

Remember, it doesn't matter how many times you mess up. God will always give you another chance. He looks at your heart, so when you sincerely want to make a change in your life, he sees that and strengthens your will to overcome.

You have a redeemer! When you make a wrong choice, ask for forgiveness. He is faithful to forgive you. He already paid the penalty for your mistakes—past, present, and future.

Life is a series of choices and God's Spirit in us is always there to help us make the right ones every time.

You need to develop a process in your mind to make your decisions based on God's Word instead of based on your emotions. Let me explain to you what I mean with this heartwarming story.

John stood up from the bench, straightened his Army uniform and studied the crowd of people making their way through Grand Central Station. He looked for the girl whose heart he knew, but whose face he didn't, the girl with the rose.

His interest in her had begun thirteen months before in a Florida library. Taking a book off the shelf he found himself intrigued,

> *You need to develop a process in your mind to make your decisions based on God's Word instead of based on your emotions.*
>
>

not with the word of the book, but with the notes penciled in the margin. The soft handwriting reflected a thoughtful soul and insightful mind.

In the front of the book, he discovered the previous owner's name, Miss Hollis Maynell. With time and effort he located her address. She lived in New York City. He wrote her a letter introducing himself and inviting her to correspond.

The next day he was shipped overseas for service in World War II. During the next year and a half the two grew to know each other through the mail. Each letter made his heart grow fonder and a romance was budding. John requested a photograph from her but she refused.

When the day came for John to return from Europe, they made plans to meet each other at Grand Central Station in New York. "You'll recognize me," she wrote. "I will be wearing a red rose on my lapel."

At 7:00 p.m. sharp, John was at the station looking for a girl whose heart he loved but whose face he'd never seen. All of a sudden, a young, beautiful woman was walking towards him.

Her figure was long and slim. Her blonde hair lay back in curls from her delicate face. Her eyes were vibrant blue. She was immaculately dressed in a flowing, white dress. She looked like an angel.

He started to walk toward her, entirely forgetting that she was not wearing a rose. She gave him a provocative smile, "Going my way, sailor?"

Almost uncontrollably he made one step closer to her, and then he saw Hollis Maynell. She was standing almost directly behind the girl.

There was a woman well past forty. She had graying hair tucked under a worn hat. She was more than plump. Her thick ankled feet were thrust into low-heeled shoes.

John felt as if he was torn in two. He wanted so badly to run after the young, beautiful woman, yet so deep was his longing for the woman whose spirit had captured his heart and companioned him with her letters.

Choices Are Simple So Don't Make Them Difficult

This would not be love but it would be something special. Maybe even better than love, a friendship that he would always be grateful for.

Reluctantly, John walked over to Hollis. "I'm Lieutenant John and you must be Miss Maynell. I am so glad you could meet me, may I take you to dinner?"

The woman's face broadened with a tolerant smile. "I don't know what this is all about but the woman in the white dress asked me to wear this rose. She said that if you asked me to dinner, she would be waiting for you to meet her in that restaurant across the street."[1]

What a great choice, one that John would never regret. He knew inside what he should do and did it. Even though it hurt, even though he wanted to follow his emotions, he chose what was right. What made him do that? Let's find out.

How do you make the right choice? How do you know what the right choice is? Sometimes it can be confusing. Sometimes what seems right can turn out to be wrong.

Unconditional love is your answer. Love should be the driving force behind every choice. The ultimate goal in life is to fulfill the greatest command God has given, recorded in Matthew 22:37-39. It says you should love the Lord your God with all your heart, your soul, and your strength. And love your neighbor as you love yourself.

Make your choice based on your love for God, yourself, and others. Love will lead you in the right direction; it is your barometer of right and wrong. When you're wavering in making a decision, ask yourself, "Is this a decision made out of love? What will be the consequences of my decision? Will my choice hurt God, myself, or others?" Your answer should be plain and simple. If it's not, when in doubt, cast it out!

John's choice was hard but simple. He knew that if he chose the young, beautiful woman he would have hurt Hollis. He knew he would regret it later. Afterwards, he would have to live with the fact that he had broken her heart. He couldn't do that. Tough decision! What do you think you would have done?

Tough decisions are made simple by applying love to the situation.

How did Moses's mother make the choice to put her baby in a basket and send him down a river? How did Joseph make the choice to forgive his brothers who threw him down a well to die? How did Mary's husband, Joseph, choose to stay with her when she was pregnant and with a child that was not his own?

> *Love always surrenders to God's will.*
>
>

They made their choices by love. Love always surrenders to God's will. First Corinthians 13 describes love. Love is patient, love is kind. Love always trusts. Love always seeks to do the best for the other person no matter what the cost.

Making your choice by love will launch you onto the road to success. You will place yourself in the arena of supernatural power, the kingdom of God. Love never fails.

CHAPTER NINE

Top Ten Choices Before You

Clearly, there are some choices that are far more important than others. That doesn't mean they are more difficult to make; it means that you should definitely take more time and thought before you make them. Keeping the goal of unconditional love in mind to guide you is critical.

The following are what I consider to be the most important decisions/choices you will ever make in your life:

- Making Jesus the Lord of your life
- Believing God's Word
- Choosing who you will marry
- Deciding what you will eat
- Choosing your thoughts
- Selecting what you will say
- Deciding how you will see yourself
- Choosing a career
- Determining to love others unconditionally
- Living to give without expectation of return

These decisions will determine your future. Each one in themselves can either make or break you. Let's briefly talk about each one and then more extensively in later chapters.

1. Making Jesus the Lord of your life will determine where you spend eternity. Letting Jesus be Lord of your life guarantees you life in heaven. Frankly, if you don't ask Jesus to be your Savior, when you die you will be thrown into a lake of fire, better known as hell. I think a good choice would be Jesus.

2. Believing God's Word gives you access to all the promises of God in the Bible. Some Bible scholars say there are more than thirty thousand. You can have them all, if you just believe. If you don't believe the Word of God, you're on your own. You will have only whatever you can do and what life deals you.

3. Who you marry is largely who you will become. The two become one in spirit which produces happiness and success. If you don't become one, you become either a divorce statistic or settle for living a separate life than your spouse.

4. What you eat will determine the quality of life you live. Eating healthful foods give you a good long life with energy and vitality. Eating the wrong foods makes you a candidate for all sorts of disease and feeling sick and tired all the time.

5. How you think determines your actions, and your actions take you where you're going in life. "As [a man] thinks in his heart, so is he" (Prov. 23:7 NKJV). If you think good thoughts in line with the way God thinks, you will have a great life. If you think negative thoughts, you'll live as a depressed, angry, and ungrateful person. Those attitudes will create chaos in your life.

6. What you say is what you will get. Your words have the power of life and death. If you speak positive, God-filled words, you proph-

esy goodness into your life. If you speak negative words full of fear and unbelief, you create the worst-case scenario in your life.

7. Your self-image encompasses how you perceive yourself and how you will perform. If you think you can't, you won't; if you think you can, you will. Your accomplishments will be in direct proportion to your self-image.

8. The career you choose becomes your life. If you choose one that you are passionate about, you will succeed and be happy. The sky is the limit. If you settle for less than what you had dreamed for, you will regret your choice and always say, "I should have…"

9. Loving others unconditionally keeps your heart pure and your mind at peace. It sets you up into the supernatural realm where the impossible is made possible. On the other hand, loving others conditionally is self-serving, controlling, and manipulative. That is how you set yourself up to fail in relationships and in business, as well as to risk the chance of never really being fulfilled in life.

10. Live to give—that's what the good life is all about. God blesses us to be a blessing. When you give with no expectation of return, you experience the highest possible joy. You place yourself in position for blessings to pour into your life; more than you can contain.

When you give expecting to get something in return, you really haven't given at all. You will always be disappointed. You will lose trust in people because they didn't measure up to your expectations, and find no true and lasting joy in your heart. You'll be bored with life, people, and your job. In short, life will feel mundane. Always searching for something to make you happy, you'll find that happiness always evades you. What a vicious cycle!

Remember, there is no condemnation in Christ Jesus. If you have made some wrong choices in your life, join the club. No one is perfect. Don't allow guilt and condemnation to lead you into another bad choice.

You've Been Set Up

Brush off those feelings of failure and disappointment. Purge your heart of regret. This is a new day and you can make it a perfect day just by your choices. You have the power. Your hold the reins in your hands. Take over, take charge, stand up on the inside, and boldly declare what you want in life.

I was sick and tired of feeling rejected, always feeling like I was less than my peers. "No one wants to be my friend," said the nagging voice I often heard. When I was in the third grade, I wanted to jump rope with the girls on the playground at school but was rejected: "No! Go play with someone else!"

I was shy, and very fearful to ever express my opinion. After all, I never had anything important to say. My self-image stunk. I was suffering from all the negative thoughts I had allowed to sink into my brain. "I'm not smart. I'm not pretty. Boys don't like me. There's nothing special about me. Nobody likes me," I rehearsed.

Everyone else had their life together but me. I never could figure out what I wanted to do. I was always trying to please everyone else, needing someone to tell me what I should do because I didn't think I was smart enough to figure it out. I always felt alone. My low self-image left me struggling with insecurity, always feeling rejected.

Thankfully, God lifted me out of that world of self-hatred. He very graciously led people into my life that spoke truth and encouragement into my life. He surrounded me with people who saw good in me. For a long time I couldn't receive their compliments, but then one day, someone I highly respected said the words that set me free.

"I want to be like you!"

"Me? Why? Are you crazy, I am nobody! If you really knew me, you wouldn't like me." Anything bad that I had ever done in my past was always there to haunt me. It could all flash in front of my mind in an instant.

Then she said it again. "No, I'm serious I want to be like you!"

Top Ten Choices Before You

At that moment, something broke inside of me. I felt as though an enormous weight was lifted out of my heart. I felt free to believe her. My mind said no but my heart said believe it! What choice was I going to make?

This was a pivotal turning point in my life. God had set me up to be free. Would I choose to live in rejection, guilt, and condemnation or believe that someone sincerely thought I was good?

Yes, I chose to believe. When I did, I allowed all hell to break loose in my heart. All the lies of the enemy came up and *out!* Rejection no longer had any power over me—I was free. Free to be me! Free to like myself! Free to say, "God has a good plan for me!"

Did those negative thoughts return and try to pull me back into rejection? Absolutely! I had to walk out my new freedom in Christ and stand on the words that had set me free. Those words have kept me free to this very day. Every day, I choose to be free.

God is always present to help us make the right choice. Take your orders from him. Don't act on your emotions or what pleases your flesh. Decide to desire the things that are pleasing to God. I know he was very pleased when I chose to believe in myself and the valuable life he has given me.

Your next choice is right now. Choose to let God do the choosing for you. Don't decide for yourself any longer. Trust the One who loves you and knows you better than you know yourself. Turn your focus to him and he will show you the way. Test him by giving him the reigns of your life. Let go of your own understanding and trust that his ways are so much greater than yours. Then you will discover that your Maker knows how to move you into the ultimate setup for your life.

CHAPTER TEN

Your Spiritual GPS

"Help! I need help! Is there anyone who can help me?"

Once when I was twelve, I made the mistake of getting on a boat with strangers just so I could go water-skiing. My girlfriend and I were at the beach and some strangers asked us to ski with them. "Sure! We'd love to," we chimed.

They looked like a nice couple, and harmless. Actually, I just wanted to ski and I really didn't care who they were. After getting in the boat and racing out to the ski zone, I started to have second thoughts. My mother, like every other mother, always told me to never go anywhere with strangers.

Now my mind started to wonder. I started to think the worst. I had disobeyed my mother without even thinking, "What could be the consequence? What could this couple do to us? What did we get ourselves into?"

The lady was the first one to jump in the water. It was my job to watch her and let the driver know when she went down. After a few rounds, she pointed her finger to her throat, making the motion to cut the throttle.

Already in fear, I made the assumption that she was telling him to cut our throats. My heart started racing. "Oh no, I'm going to die! Why did I get on this boat? Help! God, I need help! Please get me home safely and I'll never disobey my mom again," I silently implored.

Well, of course I got home safely. The lady's signal, I found out later, was to cut the engine when she was done skiing. I didn't even ski after that; I just wanted to get home. I learned a big lesson that day. I hadn't checked in with my spiritual Global Positioning System before I jumped in that boat. Fear had gripped my heart and I paid the price.

Thank God I'm around to laugh at that story today. The lessons along the road of life have taught me that checking in with God is the only way to go. His approval and guidance—my spiritual GPS—is always right on.

My friend Betsy was attending a real estate seminar and they were raffling a prize. It was a GPS. She had wanted one for quite some time, knowing how valuable it would be for her business.

She thought to herself, "I'm going to pray and ask God for me to win this prize." Boldly she prayed and exercised her authority as a believer: "Lord, I desire to have this GPS and you desire to give it to me. Thank you, Lord. That GPS is mine."

Guess who won the raffle? Betsy is the proud owner of a brand-new GPS. Her spiritual GPS, the Holy Sprit, told her how to get it. Pray and believe and you will receive, as Mark 11:24 advises. That's exactly what Betsy did and she won.

Our spiritual GPS works just like the one in your car. Global Positioning System satellites transmit signals. The GPS receivers passively receive satellite signals that transmit data which indicate information of location and current time. These signals move at the speed of light.

God's Positioning System (GPS) works by his Spirit in you who transmits signals to your receiver (heart) that indicate the direction and timing of events in your life. His signals also move at the speed of light.

The Holy Spirit is your most important GPS system. The one in your car could break down or mislead you. God's system never fails.

Your Spiritual GPS

Turn on your spiritual GPS and start using it. Life is so much easier, and you get where you want to go a lot faster. If you follow it precisely, you will never go down the wrong road. The Holy Spirit will never mislead you or leave you stranded.

He is the guiding light to your setup. He is the Counselor that advises you with knowledge beyond comprehension. He is the teacher's manual. He is the Helper who holds the world in his hand.

The Holy Spirit shows the way. God set you up to know him as your very best friend. When you allow yourself to be led by him, you will learn to expect him to meet your every need.

Gordon Robison, the director of the Middle East Media Project for the University of Southern California, said, "God meets us at the level we expect, not the level we hope."

Not long after we moved to Arizona, I was asked to be in a prestigious women's club. I was told that no one turns down the opportunity to be a member, and only a few were asked to join each year. Feeling honored, I went to the meeting.

Mesa Women's Club was very active in our community. Each year the organization planned many prosperous fund-raisers. That night, I was introduced as the new prospective member. As I stood up for all to see who I was, I felt a wave of nausea come over me.

I couldn't get rid of the knot in my stomach. "What is going on? This is such a good thing, Lord. Why don't I have peace?" I pleaded. I tried to ignore my feelings, even though I knew God was telling me not to join.

I argued with God the whole night: "Why? This is such a good thing. They help so many people. I know how to do this. I would be good at it." The next morning, I wrote my resignation letter to the club. I've learned that I can argue with God but he's always right. I'm sure I was the only one-day member in the history of that club.

At the time, I didn't know that I would become so involved in the women's ministry at our church that I couldn't have done them both. My spiritual GPS was right on and headed me in the right direction.

I was so intimidated by the GPS system in our new car! Without reading directions, I started to play with it. All of a sudden, it started to talk to me and I couldn't get it to stop. I tried pushing every button, only to get more and more frustrated. On, off, on, off—no matter what I did, I got the same annoying voice.

Why don't they make things easy? It seemed so complicated, and I didn't have the time to read the directions. Finally, by accident, I got the voice to stop. My impatience vowed to never use it again.

On the contrary, your spiritual GPS is easy to use. You're the one that does the talking. Scripture explains that "you do not have because you do not ask" (James 4:2 NKJV).

So try asking. Communicate with the Spirit of God inside of you. F. B. Meyer said, "The great tragedy of life is not unanswered prayer, but unoffered prayer." Martin Luther said, "I have so much to do [today] that I shall spend my first three hours in prayer."

Prayer is your lifeline to God. Pray, and then listen for his voice that comes out of your spirit. The Holy Spirit speaks through your conscience.

Many people say they don't hear from God (Holy Spirit). They confuse their own thoughts with the voice of the Holy Spirit. "Is that God, the devil, or me talking?" they wonder. So they stop asking because they are afraid of hearing the wrong thing.

The Holy Spirit talks to everyone who asks in faith. Faith is the key. If you're afraid, that is fear. Fear hears the voice of the enemy. What he speaks is always opposite of what God would say.

Don't ask when you're afraid of what the answer may be. Instead, ask believing that the Holy Spirit will speak truth to your heart. The Holy

Spirit will always agree with the Word of God. If you hear an answer that doesn't align with the Word, you can be assured it wasn't from God.

If it's not a word from the Holy Spirit, you will not have peace inside. The Holy Spirit is the spirit of peace and not confusion.

Far in advance, I was planning my husband's birthday celebration. He had wanted to travel abroad for quite some time, so I started to do my homework. I thought for sure we would travel to Europe. I read books, talked to friends, and surfed the Internet, trying to plan the perfect vacation.

Every time I thought I had a great plan going on, I felt so unsettled inside. I prayed for direction but I never felt peace or what I call "the green light."

Many months passed until I had to make a decision. "Lord, what should I do? You know Dennis better than I and you know the best trip for his birthday. Help! I need help!" I prayed.

Then one day I received an e-mail about a yachting adventure. I started to delete it. At that moment, a thrilling sensation swept through me. I was overwhelmed with excitement.

So I opened the e-mail and checked it out. As I was reading, the Holy Spirit spoke to my heart, "This is it!" However, I ignored his voice and went on to do something else.

As I got up to leave my computer, the Holy Spirit said, "Buy it now."

"Now? Right now? I have to think about it."

As I walked away from my computer, I felt like I was turning my back on my very best friend. I had asked for his help, but now I didn't want it. It just didn't make sense to me to go to the Caribbean, when all the while I was planning a trip to Europe.

"Trust me!" he said.

Those words pierced my stubborn heart. "OK, OK! We're going yachting in the Caribbean."

Many times we cannot understand his leading; we just need to trust and obey. The carnal mind cannot understand the things of the Spirit. If you are led by the Spirit, you can't listen to your intellect. Sometimes they don't agree. The Spirit is always right on.

Dennis had the time of his life! His birthday celebration was a memory he'll cherish forever, and I will too. But the amazing thing about God is that he had also set Dennis up.

While in the Caribbean, he made a business connection that proved out to be extremely beneficial. Doors of great opportunity opened up to him on that trip. Only God can plan a vacation and prosper you financially at the same time.

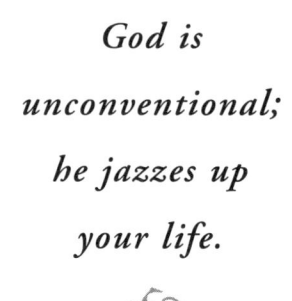

God is unconventional; he jazzes up your life.

When you yield your life and plans to him, you're opening yourself up to extraordinary happenings in your life. God can't wait to show off his goodness to you. "The eyes of the Lord search the whole earth in order to strengthen those whose hearts are fully committed to him" (2 Chron.16:9 NLT).

When you tune in to your spiritual GPS, unusual things happen. Your normal life turns into the extraordinary; standard living becomes exceptional. God is unconventional; he jazzes up your life.

Follow his leading even if it doesn't make sense. I can't imagine where we would have ended up on Dennis's birthday had I leaned on my own understanding. We would have missed out big time.

The Holy Spirit knows the truth because he is the truth. He will guide you in your true destiny, in your everyday walk of life.

The apostle John wrote, "But when he, the Spirit of truth, comes, he will guide you into all truth. He will not speak on his own; he will speak only what he hears, and he will tell you what is yet to come" (John 16:13).

Your Spiritual GPS

No more guessing games. No more missing out. No more wondering if you should or shouldn't do something. Your spiritual GPS sends you to the exact location at the perfect time. He can fast-forward the video of your life so that you will know what to expect in your future. With him, you have the advantage.

CHAPTER ELEVEN

Let Favor Work For You

I'm a planner. I love to brainstorm and come up with unlimited ideas. I like to think big and then sit back and watch God do it. When I get my faith out there, he always meets me with favor and fulfills my dreams.

Family vacations have always been important to me. I have never let the budget keep us back from making memories. God knows that my heart is into having good times with my family and he loves to give me the desires of my heart.

When our children were young, I longed to take them to Hawaii. I started dreaming and seeing us on the beach making sand castles. Then I'd see us on a catamaran, snorkeling, fishing, doing it all.

Hawaii was definitely not in our budget. Just the flight to get seven of us there was out of the question. But I couldn't get it out of my mind. "It's the desire of my heart, God, and you will make it happen," I prayed.

My husband knows that when I latch on to something in faith, typically, it will happen soon. God's favor makes a way where there seems to be no way. But five years went by, and Hawaii was not in sight.

Then an unexpected check came in the mail—there had been a mistake in our taxes. It was the first time we'd ever gotten money from the

IRS. Excitedly, I breathed, "Thank you, Lord, for your favor that gives us our heart's desire." We were on our way to Hawaii!

As Moses prayed in Exodus 33:13, we can pray, "If you are pleased with me, teach me your ways so I may know you and continue to find favor with you."

You know what pleases God? Faith. Faith in God's ability to do his will. Nehemiah pleased God. He had faith for favor, in order to move a mountain in his life. When Nehemiah heard that the walls of Jerusalem had been torn down, leaving the Jews defenseless against their enemies, he became heartsick.

Weeping for his people in their distress, he cried out, "O Lord, God of heaven, the great and awesome God, who keeps his covenant of love with those who love him and obey his commands, let your ear be attentive and your eyes open to hear the prayer your servant is praying before you day and night for your servants, the people of Israel. I confess the sins we Israelites, including myself and my father's house, have committed against you" (Neh. 1:5-6).

Nehemiah was the cupbearer to the king of Babylon. One evening the king noticed that Nehemiah looked sad and asked him what was wrong. Nehemiah was frightened to answer him, since no one was supposed to show his or her personal feelings in front of the king.

But as Nehemiah 2:3,5 records, he couldn't hold it in any longer. "Why shouldn't my face look sad when the city where my fathers are buried lies in ruins? If I have found favor in your sight, please let me go to rebuild its walls."

The king was pleased to grant Nehemiah's request because the favor of the Lord was upon him. The Spirit of God stirred the king's heart to restore the walls of Jerusalem to protect Nehemiah's people.

Nehemiah was set up by God to restore security to his nation and become the governor of Jerusalem.

Let Favor Work For You

Nehemiah had enemies on every side. He was mocked and ridiculed. Prophets were hired to intimidate him with their words. Many were scheming to kill him but Nehemiah refused to be moved and give in to fear. Instead, he prayed without ceasing. Nehemiah boldly proclaimed that God was his strength, and that God's favor would bring him success.

> *God is continually assisting you wherever you go.*
>
>

Amazingly, the work to restore the wall was completed in only fifty-two days. When his enemies heard it was finished, great fear came upon them and they lost their self-confidence. They knew that such a great achievement could only have been done with the help of the Lord. God was on their side!

Like Nehemiah, you need to expect and depend upon the favor of God upon your life. God is continually assisting you wherever you go. God is on your side!

Be on the lookout for the help you need to accomplish your dreams because God's handout is right there when you need it.

Whatever you need at the moment has already been put in place for you. It's right before your eyes. But if you are not believing for it and looking for it, you may miss it.

Be alert and favor minded. If you've asked God for something in prayer, his favor will bring it to you. You may be tempted to think, "Well, no one ever does favors for me. If I want something I have to do it myself. When I go into a store, I usually have to hunt down someone to help me find what I want."

More than likely, you are not expecting favor. You get what you expect! Change your mind and start believing for favor.

Nehemiah asked God for favor with the king, believing and expecting that God would give him what he asked for. He believed that whatever he

You've Been Set Up

> *Favor is God's presence upon you to move mountains out of the way.*
>
>

asked for in prayer he would receive because God is true to his word. God has poured out his favor upon all of his children.

That's you! If you are in sales, favor will get you in front of the right people. Favor will get you the attention of your peers. Favor will cause the bank to want to loan you money. Favor will cause your children to rise up and call you blessed, according to Proverbs 31:28.

Favor will excuse penalties even when you deserve them. Favor will move you to first-class seats when you only paid for coach. Favor is God's presence upon you to move mountains out of the way. Whatever you do, become favor minded.

One summer, my husband and I went on a ten-day road trip with our two dogs. We were traveling the Pacific Coast on the Pacific Coast Highway, from San Francisco to LA. It was a spur-of-the-moment idea; we had no hotel reservations, but didn't think it would be a problem.

Leisurely, we drove along the coastline, stopping in villages, walking beaches, and eating the local foods. We enjoyed it all. The only drawback was finding a decent hotel or motel that was pet friendly.

At the end of the day, when we were ready to crash, we had to settle for below-average accommodations because of my two darling Maltese dogs and no reservations. I reckoned that this was a road trip and the hotel was just a place to lay our heads.

By the seventh day, I found myself praying for a good hotel. "Lord, you know the kind I like (the Ritz)—a nice soft bed, fluffy pillows, room service, and a superclean updated bathroom. Please, Lord, just one night in luxury."

My husband knew what was going on in my mind, even though I had not complained… yet. I was so proud of myself.

Let Favor Work For You

When we got to Laguna Niguel, to my surprise, he pulled up to a beautiful hotel. No pets allowed. Bummer! Down the road a bit, he drove up to another great hotel. No pets allowed! Bigger bummer!

I couldn't believe it when he tried another upscale hotel. As soon as we pulled up, the valet dude ran to the car to open the door. "Checking in?" he asked.

"We hope so!" I begged. "Are you pet friendly?"

"I'm sorry, we're not."

Then he looked at the dogs, and then back to me. He paused for a moment, then quietly said, "But I think I can do something about that." He went back to the valet stand and spoke to his coworker.

Smiling, he ran back to the car. "As soon as you get in a room, we will bring the dogs up to you. Everything will be fine, don't worry about it."

Now that's favor! They made a huge exception for us. I was in heaven for the night; at least, that's what it felt like. Favor made a way where there seemed to be no way. They were inclined to bless us. And we blessed them back by staying an extra day!

Start anticipating favor. When you acknowledge God's favor, more favor is poured out on you. You get what you believe for. Declare it every day—in the morning, the afternoon, and when you go to bed at night.

Speak it out. "God's favor is upon me. He delights to give me the desires of my heart. His blessing follows me wherever I go. I am blessed when I come in and when I go out. Favor follows the sound of my voice. People are attracted to me to bless my socks off. And, I delight in doing favors for others!"

The more you declare it, the more you will experience it in your life. Be on the lookout for it and every time, make sure you give God the glory for it. Praise him and thank him every time a blessing comes your way. All good and perfect gifts come from above. Your Father delights in the

> *Anticipate an increase of favor and blessing in your life so it can flow through you to help others.*

prosperity of his children—and don't you forget it!

Don't be a fool and forget the goodness of God. Continue to praise him and love him with all your heart, soul, and strength. Don't hoard the entire blessing for yourself. Love your neighbor as yourself and give generously. Greater joy comes when you can give without any expectation of return.

When you buy dinner for someone, don't expect him or her to return the favor. Just say, "It's my pleasure!" If you bring flowers home to your wife, give them to her just because you love her. Don't expect a romantic evening. Believe me, you'll get more than you had hoped for!

Don't use God's promises to benefit only yourself. Anticipate an increase of favor and blessing in your life so it can flow through you to help others.

I love the Old Testament story of Naomi and Ruth. Usually a preacher will teach on the favor upon Ruth's life. But I love the fact that Ruth showed so much favor to her mother-in-law.

Naomi had lost her husband and two sons, one of which was married to Ruth. Naomi became depressed and bitter. At that time there was a famine in the land, so she was forced to go back to her homeland where there was food.

Naomi pleaded with her two widowed daughters-in-law to go home to their own mothers, but both were torn apart at the thought of leaving her. Ruth absolutely refused to leave Naomi.

Listen to her expression of loyalty to Naomi. "Don't urge me to leave you or to turn back from you. Where you go I will go, and where you stay I will

Let Favor Work For You

stay. Your people will be my people and your God my God. Where you die I will die, and there I will be buried. May the Lord deal with me, be it ever so severely, if anything but death separates you and me" (Ruth 1:16-17).

Ruth was determined to take care of Naomi and stay by her side through thick or thin. She vowed never to leave her as long as she lived.

Ruth laid down her life for Naomi. She moved to a foreign country, only to find herself working in the fields. Ruth tirelessly gathered stalks of grain left behind from the workers to serve Naomi dinner.

As the story unfolds, a relative of Naomi's whose name was Boaz, noticed Ruth gleaning in the fields. He had heard of her self-sacrificing love for her mother-in-law. Boaz was compelled to show favor to Ruth by keeping her safe and giving her an abundance of grain.

Boaz fell in love with Ruth. They married and Ruth gave birth to a son. They named him Obed, which means "servant of the Lord." It brings tears to my eyes when I hear the words of Naomi's friends as Ruth presented her with a grandson.

"Praise be to the Lord, who this day has not left you without a kinsman-redeemer. May he become famous throughout Israel! He will renew your life and sustain you in your old age. For your daughter-in-law, who loves you and who is better to you than seven sons, has given him birth" (Ruth 4:14-15).

Wow! That is love! Isn't that the kind of love we all desire to experience in our own lives? The undying favor that Ruth showed to Naomi is a rarity in our world today. Can you imagine being like Ruth and laying down your life for someone else?

Ruth's son, Obed, was the father of Jesse, who was the father of King David. The ultimate end of this genealogy is Jesus Christ. Ruth's favor shown to Naomi bore Naomi a grandson in her old age. Obed carried on the family line and is the ancestor of our kinsman-redeemer and Savior of the world, Jesus.

You've Been Set Up

Begin to let favor work for you by doing favors for someone else. Start with the small stuff. When you're at work, look around and find someone you could encourage. When you're finished with your job, ask someone else if you could help them with theirs.

At the grocery store, put your cart back in the slot instead of letting it slide on down the parking lot into another car. Open the car door for your wife. Fix your husband dinner once in a while. Volunteer in your community. Take someone out to dinner who can't afford it.

If you get in the habit of doing the little things, pretty soon you'll notice that favor has started to follow you around. Your heart will expand; you'll no longer feel satisfied doing the small stuff, but will dream about helping others in a greater way.

You'll want to change lives and then nations. You will constantly ask God to give you more so you can become a greater blessing to people. Then you'll be living in your setup.

God has set you up to have favor work for you. When you begin to see God's favor in your life, you will no longer doubt his goodness. You will begin to realize that he wants only the best for you and no matter what stage you are in your life, it's never too late.

You will begin to get a bigger vision for your life and start expecting doors of opportunity to open up to you. You will desire to do his good and perfect will for your life. Your purpose will be driven by love, the same kind of love Ruth had for Naomi.

Choosing to love never fails.

God's Word is full of stories exemplifying his favor. Another favorite of mine is Queen Esther and how she let favor work for her to save the Jewish nation.

Esther was a Jewish orphan who was raised by her cousin Mordecai after her parents died. Because of her outstanding beauty, she was chosen to join the harem of women who were being prepared to be presented to

Let Favor Work For You

the king for his choosing. Whoever would win his heart would become the queen of his kingdom.

Esther was chosen to enter the palace to undergo twelve months of beauty treatments—poor girl! All the while, she never revealed her nationality or family background because Mordecai had forbidden her to do so.

Esther won the favor of everyone who saw her, and because the king was attracted to her more than to any of the other virgins, he set a royal crown on her head and made her queen.

Every day, Mordecai would walk back and forth near the courtyard of the harem to find out how Esther was and what was happening to her. One day, as Mordecai was sitting at the king's gate, he overheard a plot to assassinate King Xerxes.

Mordecai relayed the plot to Esther, who in turn reported it to the king, giving credit to Mordecai. The two officials were found guilty and were hung on the gallows.

Sometime later, Haman, who was second in command in the kingdom, plotted to kill all the Jews. Haman convinced the king to annihilate all the Jews; young and old, women and children.

When Mordecai heard the news, he was bitterly distressed. He went out into the city, wailing loudly. Queen Esther sent her aide to find out why Mordecai was so upset.

Mordecai pleaded with Esther to go before the king to ask for mercy. He knew that no one could have an audience with the king unless they were summoned; Esther could be put to death unless the king extended his golden scepter. Knowing this, Mordecai still implored Esther to save their people, the nation of Israel, underscoring that God had put her in a royal position "for such a time as this" (Est. 4:14)!

Esther called a three-day fast for all the Jews and promised to appear before the king. On the third day, Esther put on her royal robes and stood in the inner court of the palace, in front of the king's hall.

The king was sitting on his royal throne. When he saw Queen Esther, he was pleased with her and extended his golden scepter. Whew!

Esther had great favor with the king; he granted her all of her requests and gave her half of his kingdom. Mordecai was recognized and honored for saving the life of the king. He became second in rank to King Xerxes. Haman was hung on the gallows for plotting to kill all the Jews.

The favor upon Esther and the wisdom of Mordecai saved the Jewish nation. They were set up for such a time as that to ensure the redemptive history of Israel—the birth of our Savior, Jesus Christ.

There is power in favor. Power to help, to heal, and to save. Let favor work through you to help a friend in need. Let favor work through you to heal a broken heart. Let favor work through you to save a life. You have the power to do these things. Step out, knowing that God's favor upon you has given you the ability to bless others.

A famous quote from Zig Ziglar, one of the greatest motivational speakers of all time, says, "You can have everything in life that you want, if you will just help other people get what they want."

That's a good way of saying "you reap what you sow," paraphrased from Galatians 6:7. Start sowing favor and you will reap favor. You will empower heaven to work on your behalf. You will employ the angels to come to your aid. You will be propelled into your setup.

Just like Esther, you were born for such a time as this. God's favor upon you can move mountains, change nations, and save lives from the power of the enemy.

Boldly confess that you are abounding with the favor of the Lord and you are full of his blessings: "Lord, you look on me with favor because I am your child. I can do all things through Christ who favors me and gives me strength. Lord, you bless me and surround me with favor as with a shield" (based on Deut. 33:23, Ps. 5:12, Phil. 4:13). That's good stuff!

CHAPTER TWELVE

Send Out Some Good Vibrations

A number of years ago at the Biltmore in Phoenix, I found myself staring at a beautiful woman having dinner with some friends. She was beaming like sunlight. I was so drawn in by her presence, I couldn't take my eyes off of her.

Her smile looked so sincere as she captivated her guests. Although probably in her sixties, out of her heart came a soft, childlike laughter.

It was almost as though I knew the kind words she was speaking by the expression on her face, even though I couldn't hear her. She exuded an atmosphere of peace and confidence. I was quite overwhelmed by her presence.

Leaning towards my husband, I asked, "Honey, did you see that woman?" I'm not usually in the habit of pointing out women to my husband, but I needed to know if he had noticed her.

"You mean that lady over there?" nodding his head in her direction.

"Yes! There's something very special about her. She's lighting up this whole place. It's very plain to see, she's got a good thing going on in her life."

Throughout dinner, I kept glancing her way. When I saw her get up to leave, I didn't want her to go. "How silly," I thought, "I don't even know her." I felt compelled to go talk to her. I jumped up from the table and told my husband I would be right back.

Making my way through the tables in the restaurant, I was wondering what I was going to say to her. I thought to myself, "Why am I doing this?" Finally, I stood right in front of her, put out my hand to shake hers, and introduced myself.

"I'm Mary June. I don't usually do this, but I just had to tell you that you light up this place. You have a glow about yourself that people can see. I can tell you are a beautiful person on the outside but also on the inside as well."

She took my hand, squeezed it, and said, "His name is Jesus!"

I knew it! That was her secret. She was in her setup! The good vibrations she emanated were a testimony of what was on the inside. Only God's presence could make someone look that happy.

> *When you have the Spirit of God, you embody the energy force that created this world.*
>
>

When you have the Spirit of God, you embody the energy force that created this world. That's a pretty powerful vibe! The restaurant lady's vibes attracted me to her. Like attracts like. Because of the law of attraction, the light that was radiating from her caused the light in me to be magnetized towards her.

Energy vibrations will attract energy of the same frequencies back to you. You need to make sure that you are continually sending out energy, thoughts, and feelings that resonate with what you want to be, do, and experience.

Your energy frequencies need to be in tune with what you want to attract in your life. If love and joy are what you want to attract, then the vibration frequencies of love and joy are what you want to create.

Send Out Some Good Vibrations

That was a life-changing event for me. I realized that I had the same power in me, the same light to attract others to Christ. She made me realize that my responsibility as a Christian was to act like one.

That night, my desire to represent my Father God to the world became the greatest priority in my heart. I realized that no matter what negative situation was going on in my life, I needed to smile and let his love flow out of me.

We all have a responsibility to let our light shine into the world. Christians should be the happiest people on earth. We are God's energy in the form of a human body.

This amazing body created by God is made up of cells which are made up of atoms which are made up of subatomic particles. Subatomic particles are energy! You are a ball of energy!

Let the truth set you free. Stop believing there is no way you can be happy. Turn your negative energy into positive. Cash in on your freedom to be happy. You have the joy of the Lord. Jesus gave you his joy so that you could be full of joy, overflowing with happiness.

> *Cash in on your freedom to be happy.*
>

Put a smile on your face; it will increase your value immediately. An American proverb says, "A smile is worth a thousand words." Those are good, positive words. If you don't know what to say to encourage someone, then just smile.

Even in the bad times, you have a reason to be happy. In James 1:2, God says to count it all joy when you face trials of many kinds. Why? Because the testing of your faith develops perseverance. Perseverance makes you grow up.

The trial you are going through is preparing you for the great things God has in your future. So laugh and tell yourself, "Pretty soon I'm going to be better off than I've ever been in my past."

You've Been Set Up

> *When you put your trust in God, he turns your battles into breakthroughs.*
>
>

There's a rainbow at the end of this tunnel. When you put your trust in God, he turns your battles into breakthroughs.

Happiness is a state of mind that sends out good vibrations. Those good vibrations engage you to your setup. Why? Simply put, your setup is extremely good. Good gravitates you into God's goodness for your life.

You are the only one that can make yourself happy; you have to make up your mind to be so. One of the greatest ways to make yourself happy is to make someone else happy. Cheering someone else up, smiling as you wave to your neighbor, giving a hug, listening to someone's idea. These are simple but sure ways to lighten up someone else's life.

When you make someone else feel good about their life, it will always make you happier about yours. You don't have to look too far to find someone who needs your encouragement. People all around you are hurting. The last person you walked by needed your smile.

We often excuse our lack of sensitivity by believing it's impolite to invade someone else's world. You may think that what the other person is going through is none of your business. Sometimes that's true, but you don't have to know all their business to give a compliment or reach your hand out to help. Our actions and deeds affect other people, many of whom we will never know.

Too many times our words and actions do not leave other people happy. We forget to keep ourselves in check and end up acting more like the devil.

I recently read an article about a school in California that changed their automated phone service after receiving many complaints from parents and caretakers. Instead of the normal, "Sorry, we can't come to the phone right now, so please leave a message," their recording said,

Send Out Some Good Vibrations

"Hello! You have reached the automated answering service of your school. In order to assist you in connecting the right staff member, please listen to all your options before making a selection:

To lie about why your child is absent - Press 1.

To make excuses for why your child did not do his work - Press 2.

To complain about what we do - Press 3.

To swear at staff members - Press 4.

To ask why you didn't get information that was already enclosed in your newsletter and several flyers mailed to you - Press 5.

If you want us to raise your child - Press 6.

If you want to reach out and touch, slap or hit someone - Press 7.

To request another teacher for the third time this year - Press 8.

To complain about bus transportation - Press 9.

To complain about school lunches - Press 0.

If you realize this is the real world and your child must be accountable and responsible for his/her own behavior, class work, homework, and that it's not the teachers' fault for your child's lack of effort: Hang up and have a nice day!"[1]

Isn't that great? If you work for a school system, you're probably thinking, "What a great idea! Let's get this on our phone." Yes, it's a little sassy, but in some ways, oh so true.

A lot of people love to complain, shift the blame, and harshly voice their own opinion. It's a belief that seven out of ten people are angry about something, ready to lash out on somebody. We've all experienced those types of explosions. Sadly, in the world today, we see it happen too often.

When you stand in the slow, long line at the grocery store, there's always that one person showing their irritation. They're swaying back and forth from one foot to the other, sighing rather loudly, rolling their eyes, looking back in the line to see if there is someone as irritated as they are. Inside, they're ready to explode. They can't hold it in any longer. Uncontrollably, they let it out, "Come on! Move it! I'll never come here again!"

How many times have you been stuck in freeway traffic? Cars aren't moving; there's been an accident. You're going to be late for work, and the boss just sent out a memo about that. Now you're sweating it.

All of a sudden, someone comes barreling past you in the gravel on the side of the road. They have had it! They're not waiting anymore. Breaking the law, they leave everyone in the dust of their raging car. Be honest, you wanted to do that, but you just didn't have enough guts.

So many people are always trying to get away with something. Think about it. How many people are fined for driving in the carpool lane with only one person in the car? How many people surf the Internet at work? How many people conveniently forget to leave a tip on the bill?

All these little things add up to the big thing—insensitivity! Being insensitive is a sure way to set yourself up to lose your own happiness.

The world has a way of polluting us. If we're not careful, we can easily become materialistic, selfish, and mundane. The vibes the world sends out are loud and clear. You cannot be a friend to them or allow them to penetrate your life.

The Bible says in James 4:4 that if you are a friend to the world, you are an enemy of God. That doesn't mean you shouldn't love the world that God created. It means that your actions should not be like those who live by the standards of the world.

Your setup is megafull of doing things to make others happy. Every day, you represent Jesus in the flesh. You are his hands and his feet to your family, friends, coworkers, and everyone you come in contact with throughout your day.

What vibrations are you sending out? Is your light shining brightly? Are people attracted to you because you illuminate God's goodness? Do you make yourself happy and stay happy?

Send Out Some Good Vibrations

Within arm's length, there is always someone who needs to be appreciated or encouraged. The people in your life need what God put inside of you to give them. The lady at the dry cleaner's, the man who owns the car wash, your mailman, the person who drives your child's school bus—they are all in your life for a reason.

You need them! Take time to think about why they just might need you. Let me tell you, they need your smile and your godly vibes.

Canadian geese instinctively know the value of needing each other. You have undoubtedly noticed that they always fly in a V formation. These geese regularly change leadership, because the lead goose needs a break from fighting the headwind which helps create a partial vacuum for the geese on his right as well as the geese on his left.

Scientists have discovered in wind tunnel tests that the flock can fly 72 percent further than an individual goose can fly.

You, too, can make people fly faster and higher than they could on their own by your encouragement, love, and support. You will always feel joy when you make someone else happy.

When you are feeling joy and a sense of expansion, it simply means you are on course. You are in your setup. The things you are focusing on, the thoughts you are thinking, the ideas you are entertaining, and the activities you are doing are moving you in the direction of your purpose, dreams, and desires.

You have activated those good vibrations, pumping your life up to the next level. And everyone around you is feeling it.

CHAPTER THIRTEEN

What My Friend the Rattlesnake Taught Me

Early one morning, I was walking down the driveway to get into my car. I had several books in my arms, well prepared for my three-hour hair appointment.

My mind was going full speed that day. We were getting ready for my son Cory's wedding. I obviously wasn't paying any attention to where I was walking because I tripped on the garden hose. Or so I thought.

Then something bit me on my leg. Startled, I jumped in fright, dropping all my books on the ground. "What was that?" I wondered. I looked down to see a huge rattlesnake slithering on down the driveway and into the desert.

I screamed hysterically, my mind frozen in panic. When I came to my senses, I ran into the house smack-dab into my two sons that had been sleeping.

"Call 911, I've been bitten by a rattlesnake!" My voice was shaky. I overheard my son Kyle in the other room on his cell phone saying, "I don't know our address, we just moved here."

> *Get God involved right now.*
>
>

"Oh great! Maybe they'll get here before I die." Why did I think that? "Stop it, Mary June! Now is the time to practice what you preach. Be a doer. Get into faith and take authority over this situation. Get God involved right now. You know what to do."

I looked down at the bite on my leg. It was bleeding but it really didn't look that bad. Then I boldly said, "According to Psalm 91:13, I can trample on poisonous snakes and they will not harm me. But please help the paramedics find my house."

After taking all my vitals, they insisted that I go to the hospital. Following a series of tests, they found no snake venom in my blood. Six hours later, they released me, amazed and perplexed.

You might ask me, "Well how do you consider that a heavenly setup? Sounds like a setup straight from hell." I agree!

But the undeniable setup was that I was prepared. I knew what I needed to do. I stepped up and took charge in the face of fear. Yes, I was afraid. My mind wanted to go to the worst-case scenario. I was tempted to give in to the fear and fall apart.

Instead, the power of God rose up inside of me and his Word came out of my mouth. The Word took authority over the situation. The outcome was a miracle and a thanksgiving to the Lord. Once again, he saved me.

The Word is our refuge in times of trouble. Every page of the Bible explains in detail what is rightfully ours. As a child of God, your inheritance gives you access to over seven thousand promises. Your Father has set you up to live a full life—of happiness, peace, joy, and prosperity.

Detailed instructions are plainly written for you to know how to receive each and every one of your God-ordained blessings. Now is the

What My Friend the Rattlesnake Taught Me

time for you to open up your eyes; dig into his Word to find the treasures that are yours. You will be amazed to find out that those things you've always wanted are already yours.

As a child of God, you have kingdom rights. When Jesus taught his disciples how to pray, he asked them to pray his Father's will into the earth. He said, "Thy kingdom come, Thy will be done in earth, as it is in heaven" (Matt. 6:10 KJV).

Jesus was asking them to pray to receive God's will into their lives. I encourage you to pray to receive and partake of all that your Father has willed to give you while you are on this earth. Bring the kingdom of God into the earth.

Jesus said, "The knowledge of the secrets of the kingdom of heaven has been given to you, but not to them. Whoever has will be given more, and he will have abundance. Whoever does not have, even what he has will be taken from him" (Matt. 13:11-12).

If you don't know what is yours, you won't get it. You will forfeit all your blessings because of lack of knowledge. Plus, you stand the chance of losing what you already have because you do not have the blessing to protect it. If you're not protected, the enemy has an open door to come in and steal from you.

We had an alarm system in our home, but after a while, we stopped using it. When we used to set it, any one of our teenagers who came in after we went to bed would set off the alarm, causing us to lie awake for hours afterward.

For various other reasons, our family was always setting off the alarm. When the bill for the monthly security fee came, we decided to turn it off. It seemed too much of a hassle at the time.

Then one night, I was home alone. My husband was out of town on business. I woke up about three o'clock in the morning feeling very sick. I

> *Jesus was saying, not many will bring heaven into earth by their faith because they are not doers of his Word.*
>
>

got out of bed, walked a few steps toward the bathroom, and collapsed to the floor. The room was spinning, and I was so weak I couldn't get up. I lay there helplessly, wondering what I should do.

It was then I glanced up to the alarm system by the door of our bedroom. It had an emergency button on it. I thought, "I need to get to that button! Then someone will get here to help me." Then I remembered—the system turned off!

Something that could have been a blessing to me was at that moment useless. Because of my former impatience and lack of knowledge, I forfeited the right to use our alarm system when I needed it. I missed out on the blessing of being protected and taken care of because I had made the choice not to use it.

Unfortunately, many treat the Word of God in the same way. You hear the Word, you know what you have, but you choose not to use it. Maybe it seems too difficult, like my alarm system. Maybe it would cause you to change and that's totally out of the question.

The truth is, you forfeit the blessing by not being a doer of the word. "Faith without works is dead," admonishes James 2:20 (KJV). You are deceiving yourself when you do not do what the Word says. Blessed is the man who hears the Word and puts it into practice. He is the wise man who builds his house on the Rock, reveals Matthew 7:24.

Jesus said in Matthew 7:21, "Not everyone who says to me, 'Lord, Lord,' will enter the kingdom of heaven, but only he who does the will of my Father who is in heaven." Jesus was saying, not many will bring heaven into earth by their faith because they are not doers of his Word.

What My Friend the Rattlesnake Taught Me

Stepping up into your setup is making yourself available to do God's will. It's a decision to humbly lay aside your own agenda. Offer yourself to your Creator to do his good, pleasing, and perfect will. When you lose your life for his sake, only then will you find your life. The set-up life of blessing.

Many Christian churches teach you how to get saved by the Word, but then stop there. They don't teach you how to get your needs met. The Word is your salvation in all areas of your life. It teaches you how to deal with depression, how to overcome an addiction, or even how to save your marriage. It teaches you the secret of living a kingdom life.

Why don't the sick get healed? Why do the poor stay poor? Why are the weary depressed and the hopeless always needy? Why does the pastor have an affair? Why do people leave the church offended? Why are strife, anger, bitterness, gossip, and slander found among the brethren?

The biggest reason is because the church is not stepping up to be doers. People hear the Word in church on Sunday and say, "Amen! Praise the Lord!" but then they walk away and never apply it to their daily lives.

"Do not merely listen to the word, and so deceive yourselves. Do what it says. Anyone who listens to the word but does not do what it says is like a man who looks at his face in a mirror and, after looking at himself, goes away and immediately forgets what he looks like. But the man who looks intently into the perfect law that gives freedom, and continues to do this, not forgetting what he has heard, but doing it—he will be blessed in what he does" (James 1:22-25).

Years ago, we were at one of our family's all-nighters at the baseball park. All four of our sons played ball. Each one of them had two or three games a week. They were on four different levels within the league: T-ball, Coach-pitch, juniors, and seniors. Each team played on a different field, but thankfully, they were all at the same park.

Not wanting to miss anything, Dennis and I would jog from one field to the next, to catch an inning with each one of the boys. To say the least,

You've Been Set Up

we spent a lot of time at the baseball park. My husband always said he could tell when they changed the brand of hotdogs at the snack stand because we ate there so often.

On this evening, the games were over and we were packing it up to head home. Jason had pitched a no-hitter and some parents were stopping us to say he had done a great job.

I heard some commotion going on behind us; someone had gotten hurt. I turned around to see what had happened. Someone was carrying a young boy in their arms and heading our way.

Simultaneously, we saw that it was our six-year-old, Patrick. Blood was spurting out of his mouth. His shirt was drenched in blood. "Oh God, what has happened?" I breathed.

My husband is good in these situations. He immediately swept Patrick up in his arms. He could see where the blood was pulsating from. Patrick had been hit in the mouth with a full swing of a baseball bat which caused his front teeth to pierce a hug gap in his top lip.

We rushed him to the emergency room, and twenty-one stitches later, we were on our way home. Thank God that's all it was! Except that it left Pat with a fat lip, and big lips weren't in yet.

Throughout his grade school years, he was called big lips. He was self-conscious about it and many times asked me if he could have plastic surgery. I agreed to it, but wanted him to wait until he was in high school.

In the meantime, I was praying for God to make his lip perfect. Why would he have to go through surgery when God could just fix it!

You guessed it. Patrick never had to have surgery. His lips are perfect. No more fat lip!

"Ask and you will receive, and your joy will be complete" (John 16:24). When you act on the Word, you always get results. Results make us happy. God loves for his children to be happy.

What My Friend the Rattlesnake Taught Me

God loves for his children to be happy, healthy, and whole. His Word holds the promise but it only comes alive when you act on it. Faith demands action. Action is acting like you already have what you believe for.

In this case, every time I noticed Patrick's fat lip, I would confess my faith saying, "Lord, I thank you that you have already healed Pat's lip. It has been completely restored to perfection, just the way you created it to be." Then I would see it done in my mind and praise God that Pat would never have to have plastic surgery. Little by little, his fat lip disappeared. Glory to God!

> *Faith demands action. Action is acting like you already have what you believe for.*
>
>

My husband and I teach a class on marriage. Many couples have problems that look ridiculously hopeless. In fact, sometimes you feel like just telling them to go ahead and get a divorce. Only because we are accountable to God, we don't advise that. But honestly, sometimes we would like to.

Some individuals are dragged to the class by their spouse. Many couples wander in looking for a quick fix for their problems; few couples are there to really commit themselves to making their marriage work. We can always tell by their attitudes and what comes out of their mouths if they are really serious about making their marriage a love story or a statistic of divorce.

The couples that hear the Word and then leave the class and apply it to their relationships are the ones who come back to us and thank us over and over again. They are so grateful to have been given the keys to having a great relationship and a marriage they truly enjoy. They are doers. They have found out the Word works.

CHAPTER FOURTEEN

Speak Up!

Blabber, blabber, yak, yak, yak. What are you speaking? What is coming out of your mouth? If you carried a recorder in your pocket to journal your conversation throughout the day, would you be pleased, disgusted, or surprised?

The way to find out who you are is to listen to what comes out of your mouth. "Out of the abundance of the heart [the] mouth speaks," discloses Luke 6:45 NKJV. Most of us would find out some things about ourselves that we weren't aware of.

Our words have tremendous power. In fact, the Bible says our words create life or death. That leads me to believe that we should seriously be wise about our conversation.

What you say with your mouth and believe in your heart will come to pass. Usually people say what they are thinking and believing to be true. With your words, you determine your attitude and set the stage for your day.

Understand, your tongue is the greatest tool you have to create your future. You are

> *You are the prophet of your own life.*
>
>

You've Been Set Up

the prophet of your own life. The words you speak are seeds that produce exactly what you say.

You must learn to tame this tool and use it properly. If you would grasp how powerful your words truly are, you could use them to get you into your setup and live out the life God has for you.

Take time to read in the book of Genesis how God created our wonderful world. The universe was created by words; God spoke it into existence. He said, "Let there be..." and it was. Merely by speaking words, God brought all things into being.

Since then, his powerful Word is holding all things together. Nothing is going to change in this world until God says so. God's in charge! He always has been and will be forever. "In the beginning was the Word, and the Word was with God, and the Word was God" (John 1:1 NKJV).

God has given us the same creative power he used in creating the universe; our words carry that power. "Death and life are in the power of the tongue, and those who love it will eat its fruit" (Prov. 18:21 NKJV).

Words are seeds that produce fruit. By deciding which words will come out of your mouth, you are choosing which fruit you want to eat during your lifetime.

When my husband lost his fifteen-year career with the newspaper, we were devastated. When the shock wore off, we found ourselves asking, "Where do we go from here? How do we start over? Can we recover soon enough not to lose our home?"

All those fearful thoughts invaded our minds. We wanted to tell everyone how unfair it was. We were victims of cruelty and longed for sympathy. When you've been treated unfairly, you want everyone to know your side of the story. Right?

> *"Trust me, I'm doing a miracle."*
>
>

Speak Up!

Only by the grace of God did something quite different happen in my heart. God gave me giant-sized faith. He put a Word in my heart that I knew would move the mountain out of the way. He said, "Trust me, I'm doing a miracle."

Immediately, I was filled with joy. There was not an inkling of fear in my heart. I knew God was doing something far beyond my imagination. He was doing a miracle and I could just sit back, rest, and wait. I had confidence that God was doing a new thing and we would end up better off than ever before.

Then, instead of talking about the situation or complaining, my confession became positive. When people would ask me what we were going to do, I would boldly proclaim, "God is doing a miracle!" I couldn't stop saying it: "God is doing a miracle!"

I didn't know what it would be. I didn't know when it would happen. I just knew God was doing it. I had no fear at all. I had total trust in the Lord.

My husband needed to hear those words. He struggled with fear and the embarrassment of losing his job. What a horrible nightmare for any man or woman to go through!

But my confession lifted him up, made him strong, and helped him keep his trust in the Lord. When I said, "Honey, God is doing a miracle," those powerful words kept him going. I said it over and over and over. It was the only confession I allowed to come out of my mouth.

The Word says you can remove mountains: "I tell you the truth, if you have faith and do not doubt…you can say to this mountain, 'Go, throw yourself into the sea,' and it will be done" (Matt. 21:21). That's exactly what I was doing; speaking to the mountains of fear, joblessness, and financial lack—the things that had no business in our lives. God had set us up for victory. He was performing a miracle!

God has promised, if you trust him with all of your heart, you will not be disappointed. He will make your thieving enemy, the devil, pay you back for all the unfair things that have happened to you. In fact, he has to pay you back seven times over. Proverbs 6:31 reveals that if the thief is caught, he must pay sevenfold, even if it costs him all the wealth of his house. God himself rebukes the devourer on your behalf, according to Malachi 3:11. Yea!

So guess what happened to us as we stood in faith for a miracle? God placed the desire in our hearts to start our own business and he enabled us to do it. We didn't realize it then, but God had set us up way ahead of time to do this. Years prior, Dennis had financially helped a friend start a safety business in Ohio. Now, in return, this same friend helped Dennis start his. We reaped what we sowed. God knew what we would need down the road, so in advance, he moved on our hearts to help a friend. Amazing!

Then he deposited in us a can-do attitude. We knew nothing about starting our own business, but we knew God as our source of wisdom. Now our confession changed to "We can do all things through Christ who strengthens us" from Philippians 4:13.

That was twenty-five years ago and God has prospered us beyond our imagination. No longer do we have to fear being demoted or losing a job. Those days are over. What could be better?

I often wonder where we would be if we had engaged in a bad confession? What if we had continued to wallow in our grief? We could have believed for the worst: "We're never going to recover. We'll be bankrupt in a few months. Let's sell the house and just try to get by. Where is God when you need him? Why did he allow this to happen to us?"

Surely, it would have ended up as a sad story instead of a success story. We would have gotten exactly what we were confessing. We would still be dealing with hardship, barely making it, mad at God, a victim to our circumstances.

Speak Up!

Imagine how that attitude would influence our children. They would be mad at God, too! Why would they want to know and serve a God that doesn't care?

Thank God, who put in my heart and in my mouth that he was doing a miracle.

Words can paint a picture of success or a picture of failure. As I inform you that God has set you up for success, what kind of picture do you see?

I believe your vision is getting bigger and bigger each time I write it. I believe your faith is growing with that vision and you are beginning to speak it over your life.

Words don't have power if they are not spoken. You have to open your mouth and speak them out. You can't just pray in your heart; you need to cry out to God.

Speak up! Tell him what you want; let your desires be known. Pour out your heart to him. Ask him to put his words in your mouth because they have the power to turn your situation around. You've got to get them out there working for you. You can't see them, but they are producing your harvest.

I'm often amazed at how smart my grandchildren are. When my first grandson, Christian, was two, he could count to one hundred and perfectly recite his ABCs. Astonished, I would say, "Christian, you are a genius!" Time and time again, he would perform for Grandma his newest skill and I would always say, "Christian, you're a genius."

Then the time came for him to go to kindergarten. During a lesson, his teacher asked him a question. "Christian, can you give me the answer?" Puzzled, he looked at her and replied, "Of course I can. I'm a genius!"

I love the power we have with our words! Today, Christian is in the sixth grade and is the number-one student in his class. Our words have the power to mold our children's and grandchildren's lives.

You've Been Set Up

As parents, we can profoundly influence our children in a positive way by our words.

Your words have the power to turn your negative situations around. Your words have the power to heal relationships and mend broken hearts. Your words have the ability to shape your future.

So speak up! Start saying what you want instead of what you already have. Start sowing seeds of life and greatness. Water those seeds every day with a good confession.

Better yet, put God's Word in your mouth. Speak it out and listen to what you say. Let it paint pictures in your mind. Allow those words to sink down into your heart. If you want to see fast change in your life, confess God's Word every day.

His Word "is living and active. Sharper than any double-edged sword, it penetrates even to dividing soul and spirit, joints and marrow; it judges the thoughts and attitudes of the heart" (Heb. 4:12-13). Let his Word change you on the inside. Then you will know his good and perfect setup for your life and be prepared to speak up and bring his will into your life.

God watches over his word to perform it in our lives. If you desire change in your life, the most powerful thing you can do is start speaking his Word out of your mouth and into your heart. God's Word is the incorruptible seed that is 100 percent guaranteed to produce.

I didn't even know what a Suburban was until we moved to Arizona. Having five children, I always drove a station wagon that we called Old Blue.

The big, spacious Suburban really caught my attention. I needed more room; not only for my children, but for all their friends that usually needed a ride. I rationalized that I truly deserved one and started on a prayer mission to get one.

We had just started our new business, so in the natural realm, there was no way we could afford it. It definitely wasn't in the budget. I knew my only hope was God—he could do anything!

Speak Up!

I knew exactly what I wanted; white with rainbow stripes around it. I saw it every day in my mind. I visualized myself driving it. Every Sunday on the way to church, I would say to my children, "Hey, did you know we are getting a new car? It's a white Suburban with rainbow stripes." I hadn't seen a car like that; I just dreamed it up in my mind.

Almost a year went by and my children began to ask me, "When are we getting this new car, Mom?" And I'd reply, "Well, it's on its way. Believe me, it's coming!"

In the meantime, our business was prospering. Dennis was unbelievably successful. Favor followed him everywhere he went. Our expectations for the business were exceeded and we knew that only God could have given us such great success.

Then the day came when Dennis said he was trading in Old Blue. Praise the Lord! For weeks he hunted for a white Suburban, but it was nowhere to be found. There were plenty of Suburbans, but no white ones.

"Honey, can you pick another color?" he asked. Hesitantly, I agreed. So Dennis was off to trade in our car. A business named Brown and Brown Chevrolet was going to give him the best deal. I was reluctantly going to be thrilled with whatever he brought home.

The following is how Dennis tells the story: When I pulled in the dealership, I parked right behind a white Suburban with rainbow stripes around it. A pleasant-looking woman got out of the car and went inside. So I got out of Old Blue and walked straight up to the salesman.

"What's going on with the white Suburban?" I asked.

"Oh, that's Mrs. Brown's car. That's why it has that great paint job [the rainbow stripes]. She's here to trade it in for her new one."

Awestruck, I asked if he could make a deal on that one.

Two hours later, Dennis pulled into the driveway with my white Suburban with the rainbow stripes! Now, what were the chances? I was elated; I knew God wouldn't let me down! My Father longs to give me the desires of my heart. And my husband does, too! God set us up!

What's even better, it was a great lesson in faith for my children. They witnessed the setup firsthand. At their young ages, they realized that God is *so good*. They learned there's nothing too difficult for God. They could pray specifically and God would do it.

You may wonder, "How did that happen? Why did God give you the desires of your heart?" It happened because I found promises in God's Word and spoke them out of my mouth.

When I confess his Word, it goes into my heart. My heart is good soil because I believe the Word. The more I speak his Word, the greater my faith becomes. My faith is the substance that brings the unseen into the natural.

When you delight yourself in the things of God, he gives you the desires of your heart. His Word says, "Seek first the kingdom of God…and all these things shall be added to you" (Matt. 6:33 NKJV).

When you fear God, you love what he loves and you hate what he hates. You won't be asking for something that will hurt you or isn't good for you. You will ask for the things that he already wants you to have. He has already put his desires in your heart.

He opens his hands and fulfills the desire of every living thing, discloses Psalm 145:16. When your heart is right before the Lord, your desires are only for good. God's desire is for you to prosper. Prosperity is the reward for the righteous.

Speak up! Get into the habit of speaking God's Word over your life. Parents, speak God's Word over your children every day. When you do, you are setting them up for success. As your children hear you, they are actually being trained in the ways of the Lord.

I have five children who love the Lord with all their heart, with all their soul, and with all their strength. In fact, now that most of them are

Speak Up!

married, I have nine children, and they all love God and serve him with all of their hearts.

Why? Because we were faithful to speak the Word of God over their lives. Every night before they went to sleep, I would pray for them and they would repeat my prayers. They would speak them out of their own mouth. Those words were ingrained in their hearts forever! Today, those words have come to pass.

What God has done for me and my family, he wants to do for you, too. Make a decision to get the wisdom of God for your life and start speaking it out of your mouth.

Find the promise in God's Word that will turn your situation around. Be diligent. Don't give up! God watches over his Word to perform it, states Jeremiah 1:12. Like Abraham, do not waver in unbelief regarding the promises of God. Be fully persuaded that God has the power to do what he has promised.

When trials and troubles came into our lives, and believe me, with four boys we had some trials, we taught them to totally rely on God to get them out of trouble. They have witnessed the favor of God, and his goodness and mercy has covered them, time and time again.

They have learned to speak life to their dreams and to avoid negative talk that kills their seed. They know what they say with their mouths and believe in their hearts will come to pass.

If you're always talking about your problems, you're always going to have problems. And talking about them will make them grow. If you're always complaining about this ache and that pain, you will continue to stay sick. If you're in the habit of talking down to your mate, you'll never have a meaningful relationship.

Your words create your life. The Bible compares our words to the rudder of a ship. Although ships are large and driven by strong winds, they are steered by a rudder wherever the pilot wants to go. Likewise, the tongue is a small part of the body but it controls the course of our lives. We need to learn how to tame the tongue and bring it into line with the Word of God.

Speak up right now and boldly declare what you want in life. Notice the power of your words when you state Bible verses as fact: "I am a child of God and heir of all the blessings in Christ Jesus. I am the head and not the tail. I reign in this life by Jesus Christ.

"I am more than a conqueror. I can do all things through Christ that strengthens me. God blesses me with every good thing and grants my heart's desire. I am prosperous and in good health because my soul is prospering by the Word of God."

Go to the Word and find the promises you need in your life. There is something for everything you will ever need in this life. God set you up for success by giving you his Word to put in your mouth. So speak up!

CHAPTER FIFTEEN

Divine Connections

In 1999, I was in charge of the women's ministry at our church. We were planning our upcoming women's conference and praying about who we would invite to speak. One of my favorite TV evangelists at the time was Joyce Meyer. I felt like she was always preaching directly to me. It seemed like she could read my mind, or as if she had walked in my shoes.

I mentioned to the conference team to start praying and believing for Joyce to be our guest speaker. At that time, our church was just approaching about fifteen hundred people and our women's conference would bring in about three hundred women. To have Joyce Meyer come to our conference was a huge step of faith.

One morning, I heard on the radio that she was speaking at a church in a nearby city. I thought to myself, "I will go there and see if I can get close to her. Then I could ask her in person to be our guest speaker."

Several weeks later, I went to that church where Joyce was speaking. It was packed out and she was nowhere in sight. Everything was roped off and you couldn't get to the front of the church. They were protecting her from being bombarded by hundreds of people just like me.

Before the meeting started, I thought I better go to the restroom. As I was walking down the hallway, I was praying that God would make a way where there seemed to be no way to meet Joyce.

I was totally into my prayer and thoughts. I found the restroom and was actually going into the stall when bam! I walked right into a woman much taller than I. "Oh, I'm sorry!" I stuttered. Then I looked up and saw that it was Joyce Meyer!

I was flabbergasted. I quickly came to my senses and said, "Oh! You are Joyce Meyer."

"Yes," she said.

Then I blurted out, "I've been praying that I could meet you so I could invite you to speak at our women's conference this year. Would you come?"

Joyce gave me a very strange look. It took her a moment to answer me. Then to my amazement, she said, "Yes, I will. Call my office tomorrow and talk to my secretary. I will let her know you're calling."

Just like that, it happened! I was in shock. I could hardly listen to her message that night because I was so in awe of what God had done for me. He totally set me up and gave me the desire of my heart. I just kept praising him and thanking him for his goodness and love.

Another obvious setup! What are the chances of that happening? God did it. His timing was perfect to get me to walk right into that divine connection.

I realized later that the reason Joyce hesitated when I asked her to come was because she was checking in with God. God immediately told her yes!

A couple months later, Joyce Meyer was the speaker at our women's conference. Everyone was extremely blessed. God had made it happen, and had gone beyond my dreams. Today, Joyce Meyer will only speak for audiences of ten thousand or more.

Divine Connections

God wants you to realize that every blessing comes from him. He wants the credit for your successes. He's your hero who sets you up to win in life. He is a good God, all the time.

He has already set your life on course. Your divine connections are already in place for your advantage. Everything around you exists for your benefit. You need to use it and enjoy it.

Do not forfeit the things that God has put in your life to make your life work. Open your eyes and see the big picture.

It is God's desire to make you into a great nation, just as he did to Abraham. You are the seed of Abraham and heir of his blessing. God's heart is set on making your name great.

It grieves the heart of God when you ignore him. He is constantly talking to you and unceasingly trying to get your attention. God will never stop trying to get you to notice his influence and direction for your life.

Realize that faith is not hard. It's all about having the faith of a child. "Unless you change and become like little children, you will never enter the kingdom of heaven. Therefore, whoever humbles himself like this child is the greatest in the kingdom of heaven" (Matt. 18:3-4).

Children are trusting and unpretentious. They believe what you tell them. They are open to learn and do what you ask them. They know they are small and adults are big. They know who runs the show.

God runs your show. Take on the perspective of being his little child. If you humble yourself into this position with your Father God, you will launch yourself into greatness. You will actually put yourself in the right place at the right time and walk right into your divine connections. Get ready to move on up to the good life!

Early on, we all believed in Santa Claus. Even today, when I watch *Miracle on 34th Street,* there is something in me that wants to believe again. It's the kid in me.

You've Been Set Up

> *There's a switch in your brain called the chooser. You can turn it to the believe mode at any moment.*
>
>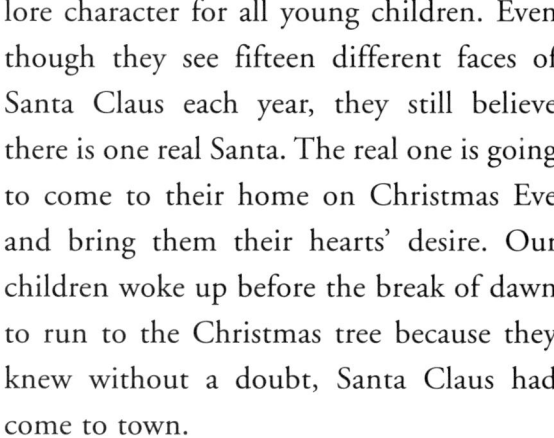

Santa Claus is the most believable folklore character for all young children. Even though they see fifteen different faces of Santa Claus each year, they still believe there is one real Santa. The real one is going to come to their home on Christmas Eve and bring them their hearts' desire. Our children woke up before the break of dawn to run to the Christmas tree because they knew without a doubt, Santa Claus had come to town.

We all believed because we wanted to believe and we trusted our parents' word. As children, we believed in Santa Claus with excitement and expectation. I think that is what God is looking for—"Don't ask questions, just believe! Believe my Word!"

There's a switch in your brain called the chooser. You can turn it to the believe mode at any moment. When incoming information is contrary to what you believe, the breaker flicks the switch off. But all you have to do is reset the breaker to turn it back on. I encourage you to take a second to do that.

Within twenty-four hours of bumping into Joyce Meyer in the restroom, my breaker flicked my switch off several times. On the way home from the meeting that night, I started to think that when I would call her office they would have no idea who I was. "She's going to have second thoughts and decline the invitation. Maybe she just said yes to get me out of her way in the bathroom," I imagined. Then I caught myself, "No, no, no! Stop that unbelief!" I reset my breaker.

I struggled again the next morning, thinking, "Joyce will probably change her mind once she realizes we are a small group of women. She doesn't know her schedule and there will be a conflict." On and on, the negative thoughts kept invading my faith. Once again, I caught myself. "*Stop!* Get back into believing! Turn the switch back on to believing." Again, I reset my breaker.

We all struggle with doubt and unbelief. Don't feel like you are the only one or think it's impossible to overcome. Nothing is impossible with God. He turns impossibilities into realities. That's why we need him! When God does the work, it's a sure thing.

When doubt and unbelief seem bigger than our faith and we can't get the switch to reset, what can we do? Well now it's time to go on a fast. I know your flesh didn't like that, but sometimes the truth hurts. By studying Joel 2 and Isaiah 58, you can get a good idea of what fasting will do for you. Fasting and prayer breaks the stronghold of unbelief and releases mustard-seed faith. Matthew 17:21 connects prayer and fasting with overcoming unbelief, or in other words, feeding your faith and starving your doubts.

Jesus explained to his disciples, "If you have faith as small as a mustard seed, you can say to this mountain, 'Move from here to there' and it will move. Nothing will be impossible for you" (Matt. 17:20-21).

A mustard seed is one of the smallest seeds on earth; so small, you really can't see it with the naked eye. Thousands of them would fit into a pinhead. Yet, the smallest of seeds becomes a great big tree.

God has given us all a measure of faith. Our faith starts out small; God wants us to try it out and see that it works. When we act on our faith and get the results we've prayed for, our faith increases. Faith grows in our hearts and occupies more space, squishing out doubt and unbelief. You can believe for

> *Faith grows in our hearts and occupies more space, squishing out doubt and unbelief.*
>
>

bigger things as your faith grows. Even though in our minds we might consider some things bigger than others, nothing is too big for God.

Step into faith for divine connections. Ask God to open your eyes to see the big picture of your life. Be grateful for the people he has placed in your life and appreciate them as blessings. Believe for favor with all men. Believe for God to speak to you and guide your footsteps. You will be amazed by the way he will move in your life and set you up on top.

CHAPTER SIXTEEN
The Amazing Power of Belief

*There is only one success—
to be able to spend your life in your own way.*
—Christopher Morley

What you believe about yourself is more powerful than what anyone else around you believes. Believe that you can accomplish whatever you desire. As the Word of God in Romans indicates, if God is for you, who can be against you?

Abraham believed God and had a child when he was ninety-nine years old. Noah believed God and built an ark to save his family and the world. Joseph believed God and became the ruler of Egypt after being sold as a slave.

Gideon believed God and defeated his enemies with a few men and no weapons. Samson believed God for supernatural strength to tear down the temple of the Philistines with his own hands. Paul believed God to peach the Word to the world powers of his day and to write most of the New Testament.

The Word of God is full of true stories of heroic acts of faith by ordinary people who chose to "just believe." Now it's your turn to believe.

You've Been Set Up

Heb 11:1 says, "Faith is being sure of what we hope for and certain of what we do not see."

There's a story in the book of Mark about a dad named Jairus. His twelve-year-old daughter was dying. Jesus just happened to be in town. Seeing Jesus, Jairus fell at his feet and pleaded with him to come and lay his hands on his daughter so that she would be healed.

When Jesus was on his way, some friends of Jairus's stopped to tell him that his daughter was already dead. Hearing this, Jesus turned to Jairus and said, "Don't be afraid; just believe" (Mark 5:36).

Just believe, Jairus! No matter what it looks like, just believe! Don't lose faith now. Breakthrough is a minute away. Jairus obeyed Jesus—he believed—and his daughter was healed.

Do you see the setup in this story? Jesus was there. Jairus knew about Jesus. Jesus knew the girl had died. When Jesus spoke the Word to Jairus, all fear and doubt left. Jairus had to stay in faith so Jesus could heal his daughter. Those two words, "just believe," had the power to raise the dead.

No matter what your life looks like right now, if you will just believe God has set you up, your faith will cause supernatural things to start happening in your life. Start believing that you can do great things.

It's a sure thing! You were made to possess the fatness of the land. Prosperity is your reward. Gifts come overflowing into your hands. Doors of great opportunity are constantly opening up to you.

After my children were out of high school, we decided to move out of the neighborhood that we had lived in for fourteen years and build a new house. Sounded like fun, a new adventure, and we were ready for a change. We knew the neighborhood where we wanted to live. The lots had great views of the city lights. So we put in a bid on one of the lots with a contingency that our home would sell.

Isn't it funny how you fix up your house when you're getting ready to sell it? We painted, cleaned out, threw away, and replaced things that were

The Amazing Power of Belief

broken. Our home was in tip-top shape. It looked so good, we almost decided to stay. But it didn't sell.

Eventually, we lost the lot. Someone came along with cash and bought it. Bummer! We were back to square one, looking for a lot to build on. I never realized how important this decision would be. Maybe we would be living in this house for the rest of our lives, so we better love the location, right?

Months went by and we still had not found a lot. We were so busy with work, family, sports, and other activities, it was hard to find time to look.

Every once in a while, I would drive through the neighborhood with the city lights, to see if anything new was on the market. One particular morning, I drove by the lot that we had lost to see if the owner had started to build.

For the first time, I noticed the lot across the street. There wasn't a sale sign on it but it was vacant. It was a large, beautiful, sloping lot at the base of a mountain. I stopped the car and just sat there. Unconsciously, I started to pray, "Lord, I love that lot. It's better than the one we lost. Help me find out who owns it and let it be for sale."

Just then a gentleman walked by my car. I rolled down the window and said, "Excuse me, sir. Do you know who owns this lot?"

"Yes, I do," he said.

"Oh! Is it for sale?" I asked.

"No," he said, "I am planning on building on it myself."

"Well, would you think about selling it?"

The gentleman looked at me strangely, then said, "OK, I'll think about it."

We exchanged phone numbers and I told him we would call him in a couple of days. I decided to just believe that this man would have a change of heart and decide to sell his lot to us. We prayed, believed, and expected it to happen. I knew it would be a miracle because this lot had the best view in the neighborhood.

I could hardly wait for the days to go by. Three days later, I sat on the edge of my chair while my husband made the phone call. As my husband was talking to the gentleman, he started to smile and nodded his head at me. I knew what that meant—it's a go! The man was selling his lot to us!

A few weeks later, the deal went through and the lot was ours. Thank you, Lord! When you just believe, miracles happen.

It wasn't a coincidence that I just happened to be sitting in front of that lot when the owner walked by. Furthermore, the owner must have been teetering back and forth about building. The timing was perfect. God set me up. He wanted us to have the best. He always goes beyond what you believe for. He gives you the desires of your heart and more.

Even if you cannot see your setup right now, start believing you have one. When you apply the keys that I am sharing with you in this book, you cannot miss it. God is faithful! He is sitting on the edge of his throne, waiting to see if you will just believe.

The plan God has for your life is beyond what you can conceive. His ways are so much greater than our ways and his thoughts are much bigger than ours.

All the things that are important to you are important to God. When you let him be in charge, you don't have to fear giving up anything. You gain with God. He's a God of increase, not decrease.

After God had miraculously supplied us with the beautiful lot, we began to think about what kind of home we would build. Spending hours at the bookstore was worthless. We needed to visually see a home that would strike us as the one.

One Saturday, we headed out to find the house. Our only plan was to head towards Scottsdale, and with God in charge, he would have to do the rest. During the drive, I prayed out loud. "Lord, please lead us to the

The Amazing Power of Belief

house you want us to build. You know what we would love, so just show us the one."

We drove for about forty-five minutes and headed towards some mountains. We were drawn to a particular gated community. We pulled up to the gate to find a guard. He asked us whom we were coming to visit. "We are looking at a house," we said. He let us in.

We drove around for maybe five minutes when I saw it. I saw the home we were supposed to build. It was sitting on a lot just like ours. It would be perfect and it was beautiful.

"Stop the car, honey, this is it!" There was complete silence as we both sat there admiring the home. It wasn't completely finished. "Let's go through it!"

We walked up the long driveway to the house and glanced over to one of the workers. "Can we go through the house?"

He was Spanish. He nodded his head yes.

As we entered the front door, overwhelming joy entered my heart. It was exactly what I had dreamed about and more. The layout of the home was perfect. We were in awe of the architecture and unique ideas they had incorporated. We fell in love with the home. It was amazing.

During our self-guided tour, we bumped into a young man who held out his hand and introduced himself as the owner of the house. Busted! We had no clue he was there. Sensing our embarrassment, he laughed and told us he took it as a compliment.

He graciously made us feel comfortable, giving us a guided tour of his home, explaining every detail. He disclosed the fact that he had spent two years with an architect and eighty thousand on the plans.

"Are you serious?" I was in shock. "Is that what it takes?"

After a long conversation, Dennis exchanged business cards with him and then we left.

I couldn't get the home off my mind. It was perfect for us and also for the lot we were building on. But how would we get the plans?

If God led us there, he must have a plan. God was in charge.

Prayer was our only option. And what did God say? "Call the owner and ask him for the plans." Why didn't we think of that? We would pay him for them.

We called him and offered to pay for the plans, but he refused. He refused to take any money because he wanted to give them to us for free! "I will bring them to you," he said. The next day, the plans arrived at our front door. Unbelievable! We were given plans to build our dream house for free.

How does that happen? We were set up. When you let God be in charge, he will get it done. He will never let you down. He is a Father who is longing to bless his children. God is so good. He will not withhold any good thing from you. He is loving, generous, and fair to all of his children.

"How great is your goodness, which you have stored up for those who fear you" (Ps. 31:19). God is good, gracious, and merciful. He lavishes his goodness upon us by his own free choice.

Many find it almost impossible to believe that someone could love us so unconditionally and deeply, to give us all things completely free.

Now is the time of no limitations. Now is the time for you to carry out the plans of God. You are called to display his glory in the earth. Your life was designed to touch the world with his love. You have been blessed to be a blessing. The only way your neighbor can get a taste of God's goodness is by your willingness to share it.

It's God's pleasure to bless you. He wants to pour so much of his goodness into your lap that you are weighed down. God's desire is for you to have the ultimate experience of life on earth. You are blessed in the city and in the country. The Lord sends blessing on everything that you put your hands to. Your descendants are blessed. All your possessions are blessed. The Lord has made you the head and not the tail. You are always at the

The Amazing Power of Belief

top and never at the bottom. The blessing comes upon you and overtakes you, all according to Deuteronomy 28:2-4, 11-13. Hallelujah! God has set you up to have heaven on earth.

One of my favorite hotels is the Ritz Carlton. I love to stay there because the staff treats you as if you are royalty. They are experts at making you feel warm and fuzzy and welcomed. They bend over backwards with kindness, doing unexpected favors that make you feel honored to be their guest.

Coming and going they greet you, having memorized your name, bowing down as you walk by. "Good morning, Mr. and Mrs. Collins! Have a great day!" And upon returning, "Welcome back, Mr. and Mrs. Collins!"

"Thank you!" we humbly reply.

Then comes their famous, "It's my pleasure!"

Wow! I love that! They really want me to be happy. Their hearts are so sincere. They have me convinced that I am worthy of their royal treatment. It's their pleasure to do anything for me. It's crème de la crème all the way, when you stay at the Ritz.

That's the way God is. When you ask him for something, he says, "It's my pleasure!" It's God's pleasure to give you every good thing. He has given us the world and everything in it. If you can't believe that's the truth, you simply need a revelation of the goodness of God.

Ask God to give you the spirit of wisdom and revelation so that you may know him better. Ask him to open up the eyes of your heart so that you may know what he has

> *Your best life is a gift from your Creator. It is an undeserved handout that comes from his goodness and mercy so that he might express his great love for you.*

called you to do in this life. Ask him to reveal to you what you have inherited as a child of God and the power he has given to you to use for his purposes, all according to Ephesians 1.

The amazing truth is God's favor and blessings are completely free. Your best life is a gift from your Creator. It is an undeserved handout that comes from his goodness and mercy so that he might express his great love for you.

You can walk every day of your life in your setup of blessing and purpose that God has prepared for you. Don't settle for good when he's already given you the ultimate best. Grasp the truth: God has made you for a purpose that is very magnificent. Just believe!

Understand, you can't do it without him. With God, your destiny is discovered and passionately comes alive within you. Through a relationship with your Maker, you will live out your dreams. Your life will become a love story.

You will no longer be separated or foreign to the abundant life. You will be hooked up to your covenant promises Christ died to make real to you. You will no longer be without hope in a world of your own, living by chance. You will live out God's perfect will for your life. A life that is too good to be true.

Abundance is not something we acquire; it is something we tune into. Author Wayne Dyer said, "There is no scarcity of opportunity to make a living at what you love; there's only scarcity of resolve to make it happen."

Man's carnal mind cannot comprehend the goodness of God or the magnitude of what he has freely given to us. You must focus on the fact that, with God, there is no lack. He is able to meet all your needs according to his riches.

This universe was equipped by him to supply you with abundance in all things. Those things flow into your life from the life giver by believing. Stop entertaining limiting thoughts and start believing for what you want. What you want will show up when you're faithful to just believe!

CHAPTER SEVENTEEN
Bloom Where You Are Planted

Have you ever asked yourself, "Why am I stuck in this situation? How did I end up here? Where could I go to escape these challenges? Doesn't God have more for me? If this is what I'm supposed to be, God made a mistake."

Be honest and say yes. Life isn't fair, and you know it. Everyone has been dealt a bad hand. You're going to have bad days every once in a while. So just accept them and move on. Bad days are a part of life.

If you seem to have lost your motivation, your job is boring, there is no room for promotion, and you are irritated with the people you work with, don't give up. During those times, the seducement of the enemy is right there to tell you to throw in the towel and move on to something better. But you need to hang in there. Something is about to change.

American naturalist and essayist John Burroughs said, "The lure of the distant and the difficult is deceptive. The great opportunity is where you are."

Joseph was dealt a bad hand when his own brothers tried to kill him but instead sold him as a slave to the Midianites. Joseph was only seventeen years old when he found himself living with strangers in a foreign country. Overnight, he went from being a spoiled shepherd boy to a servant of the enemy.

The Bible says the Lord was with Joseph and he prospered. Obviously, Joseph's relationship with the Lord gave him the strength and wisdom to make the best out of his life, right where he was.

The way in which Joseph lived his life gave evidence that the Lord was with him. His Egyptian master recognized that Joseph had an attitude of excellence and integrity. Everything that he set his hands to do was so blessed that Potiphar put him in charge of everything he owned.

Joseph's reaction to his new life as a slave could have been so different. He could have thrown himself into fits of anger or rage or succumbed to bitterness and depression. He could have tried to escape. He could have thought to himself, "Life is not worth living if I have to be a slave. Just let me die!"

Instead, Joseph decided to bloom where he was planted. He made a choice to live a life pleasing to the Lord, trusting that his God would reward him for his obedience. And that's exactly what happened. Joseph was highly favored and honored as a faithful slave to his Egyptian master. Eventually, he became second in charge over all of Egypt.

> *If you don't like where you are, open your eyes and see a different picture.*
>
>

Most likely, you are right where you are supposed to be. God planted you there for his divine purpose. Moving to a new destination or turning in a different direction will not solve your problems; they will go with you and the detour will cost you time and money.

If you don't like where you are, open your eyes and see a different picture. The grass always looks greener on the other side of the fence. Remember, the grass is only

Bloom Where You Are Planted

greener because they have watered it more and maybe even thrown on some fertilizer. Decide to bloom where you've been planted.

Find the blessing in your challenge. In the midst of trials, there's a setup waiting for you to discover. Change your attitude towards the people in your life; they're in your life for a reason. Ignore your circumstances—if you don't like them, don't worry because they are subject to change at any moment.

Add something fun and exciting to your life to get your mind off the negative. Don't put another log on the fire by moaning and groaning about it. Your life cannot be seen through negative eyes.

Currently, one of the most popular action/drama series on TV is called *24*. The hero, Jack Bauer, is on a quest to protect the United States from terrorism. The entire series happens in a twenty-four-hour day. Each episode covers one hour of real time as viewers watch Jack Bauer walk through another astonishing day.

In that one hour, Jack encounters many major life-threatening situations. From poisonous gas to atomic bombs, his life is always on the line. Jack is always set up to fall right into the hands of the terrorists.

Even though you know he is going to escape because the show must go on, you are on the edge of your seat wondering how he is going to get himself out of this mess. Jack always figures out the setup in his ingenious way of taking advantage of all the resources around him to escape the enemy and save the country once again.

Maybe you are wondering why you are where you are. You're constantly asking yourself if you're doing what you should be doing. If so, there's one thing you must do to make those tormenting questions stop.

Humble yourself and make the decision to be content in any and every situation. Don't let your heart be troubled. Trust in God and he will fill your life with the resources to succeed in the place where you are right now. God will open your eyes to see the opportunities that are right in front of you. He has set you up to bloom where you have been planted.

Because three of our sons were stepping up and running our safety company, Dennis was on the lookout to invest in another business. Dennis's role had become more of a mentor instead of a daily manager. He was feeling the need to be more involved in a different business so he could let his sons take over the ship.

During this time of transition, many questions and feelings came to the surface. "What's next? What would I enjoy doing? Maybe I should be retiring. Where do I start looking? I don't want to make a mistake at this time in my life," he pondered.

It is always difficult to move on to something new. Feelings of fear and doubt try to creep in. Walking away from the business he started twenty-five years earlier put a lump in his throat and tears in his eyes. But he knew it was time to move on so his sons could have the opportunity to take the business to the next level.

Now, in limbo, Dennis had to trust God's leading. He had absolutely no idea what it would be. He just kept his eyes and ears open and was diligent to research many different avenues of business. He faithfully read the Word for encouragement and direction. Together, praying the Word over our lives and future ignited our faith as we patiently waited for an answer.

One day, a friend of his asked him to go to lunch. His friend was having some challenges with his own business and wanted some advice from Dennis. During their time together, his friend disclosed another business that a group of men had started a few months prior.

This got Dennis's attention. He asked many questions. As the conversation went on, he felt an excitement welling up on the inside of him and the desire to know more about this new company. Then he asked, "Are they interested in another investor?"

Riding back from the luncheon in the car, Dennis prayed and asked the Lord if this was what he was supposed to do. Immediately, he was filled with the anointing. The anointing is a *yes!* from God. It's an overwhelming knowing in your spirit that you are doing the right thing.

A few weeks later, Dennis became a partner with this new company. It has been an interesting challenge, a stretch, a blessing, and a life-changing growth—mentally, spiritually, and financially. Dennis walked right into his setup as he trusted God right where he was. Once again, he is blooming where he is planted.

You may be thinking that just sounds too easy. With God, it is easy. He doesn't want you to waste time doing the wrong thing. He wants to plant you and see you grow beyond your imagination.

Too many times we get anxious and impatiently make a choice for ourselves—a dissatisfying choice that goes nowhere in a hurry.

If the answer to your problems are obvious to others but you can't seem to figure them out on our own, maybe you really don't want a solution. Maybe you are more bent on escaping, than on accepting the truth that God has you right where he wants you. You just need to start blooming!

In times of transition, you can feel so fruitless. There are seasons for rest when we feel misplaced. But God is growing you up for the next big adventure in him. He's planting more seed in you to blossom in season.

We can learn so much about ourselves and the choices we make from reading about the characters in the Bible. Their stories reveal God's setup for each one. How they

> *If the answer to your problems are obvious to others but you can't seem to figure them out on our own, maybe you really don't want a solution.*
>
>

You've Been Set Up

found it, moved in it, and bloomed. Their stories also reveal things they didn't do and things they should have done. God cast them and placed them on the scene exactly where they should have been.

He set them up to do his will, but each one got off course a little, only to be set back in place. Eve was the first to eat the forbidden fruit, but she wasn't the last. Every page of the Bible holds stains of forbidden fruit upon it, such as those of Abraham lying about Sarah, or Peter lying about Christ. Nonetheless, the Bible is a story of how God uses characters to accomplish his purpose right where there are.

Take a look at King David's life. He was so full of ups and downs; he was a mountain range of peaks and valleys. He had an enduring inconsistency about him where his heart longed for God but his behavior just didn't always catch up.

David was a man of peace but with blood on his hands. He was faithful to his friends but had one of his soldiers murdered. He dealt with many different emotions that you can read about in the psalms he wrote.

It's easy for most anyone to relate to David. Even in the midst of all his inconsistencies, he still is known as the man who had a heart for God. And that's what God is looking for. Someone who knows in their heart they are not perfect but are perfectly loved by their Savior.

> *Someone who knows in their heart they are not perfect but are perfectly loved by their Savior.*
>
>

Because of his perfect love for you, God has planted you in a favorable position for your life and growth. He has provided opportunities all around you for your advantage. He wants you to bloom where you are planted. So anticipate the revealing of his plan. In faith, stand and be patient, for God will reveal it.

Bloom Where You Are Planted

In the meantime, pray and listen! Be alert and look around you. The people in your life are keys to your destiny. Your job is a stepping-stone to your purpose. Your family is a mirror that reflects who you are. Your friends are a picture of where you are going. Step aside and look at the big picture with God. He will reveal things that you've never seen before.

Find the hidden objects in the picture. A game that is always on the back of the children's menu in restaurants instructs players to do so. How many animals can you find in this picture? My grandchildren usually find them before I do. Just when we think we have found them all, someone finds another one.

That's how it is with the big picture of your life. Just when you think there's nothing more to do—I'm stuck, there's no way out, my life is a mess—God points out the hidden blessing. The missing link to what you've always wanted. The dream that never happened. At last, the impossible has been solved.

> *Just when you think there's nothing more to do—I'm stuck, there's no way out, my life is a mess—God points out the hidden blessing.*
>
>

This new link has been there all the time. You just needed God to point it out to you. Now, new hope feeds the seed that God planted in your heart when he formed you in your mother's womb. Destiny begins to grow. You're doing the thing you were meant to do. You're blooming and the fruit is sweet.

Moses was shocked when God asked him to lead the Israelites out of Egypt. He begged God to send someone else, saying something along the lines of, "I am not qualified to do this. I am not your man."

God would not let Moses deny his destiny. I can hear him saying, "Moses, you've been set up to do this! I planted you in Egypt even though

You've Been Set Up

you were born an Israelite. You know the ropes. You rubbed shoulders with the big guys. They even liked you until you killed one of their own. This is your deal. You're the man."

God has a deal set up for you. When he formed you in your mother's womb, he planted a destiny seed in your heart. God richly supplied the soil of your heart with all the nutrients needed to make that seed produce a bountiful harvest. God also placed a yearning in your heart to love him forever.

Then he determined the timing of your birth and where you were to be born. You have been masterfully set in the ideal surroundings for your maximum growth and happiness. God doesn't make mistakes. You are meant to bloom where you have been planted.

Have you ever thought about why you were born where you are? Or why you are here now and not born in the seventeen hundreds? It's because the Creator intended for you to be here now! You are a part of his master plan for this age, time, and place.

> *You are not a misfit; you are the ideal model.*
>
>

You are not a misfit; you are the ideal model. God hit the bull's-eye when he made you. The book of James tells us to humbly accept the Word planted in us. That Word is your destiny. God's divine decree for your life has been planted in you. He intends for you to know it and do it with zeal and passion.

CHAPTER EIGHTEEN

Love Connection

The world is waiting for you to change it by your love. Little ole you can make the biggest difference with the smallest act of kindness.

A story I read reveals the kind of love I am talking about. It's called "The Hairbrush Experience." International Bible teacher, Beth Moore, was waiting to board a plane. Minding her own business, or at least she thought, she had her Bible out on her lap for a last-minute study. Glancing up for a moment, she couldn't help but notice an old man in a wheelchair sitting across from her; humped over, skin and bones, dressed in clothes that were twice his size.

She couldn't help staring at him, noticing his stringy, gray hair hanging well over his shoulders and partway down his back. His fingernails were long, but clean. He looked like a lonely, pitiful old man. "Where could he be going? What was his story?" she wondered.

As much as Beth tried to ignore him, her heart began to ache with compassion. She knew that within her the heart of God wanted so badly to reach out to him. She

> *The world is waiting for you to change it by your love.*
>
>

immediately began to resist the prompting of the Spirit and started to argue with God in her mind.

"Oh no, God. Don't ask me to witness to this bizarre-looking old man in front of all these gawking people."

Then she heard the still, small voice inside her spirit say, "I don't want you to witness to this man. I want you to comb his hair."

Those words were so clear to Beth. Her heart leaped into her throat. "What? Oh Lord, I will witness to this man right now. What difference does it make if his hair is a mess?"

Again, God clearly spoke to her heart and said, "I don't want you to witness to him, I want you to go brush his hair."

"But I don't have a hairbrush," she argued.

Beth knew she had to obey God. Slowly she got up from her seat, walked over and knelt down in front of the man. She asked, "Sir, may I have the pleasure of brushing your hair?"

To which he responded in volume ten, "If you expect me to hear you, you're going to have to talk louder than that!"

Beth took a deep breath and blurted out, "Sir, may I have the pleasure of brushing your hair?"

At that point, every eye in the vicinity was on the two of them. The old man looked up to her with absolute shock on his face and said, "If you really want to."

"Yes sir, I would be pleased. But I have one little problem. I don't have a hairbrush."

"I have one in my bag," he responded.

As Beth began to comb his hair, a miraculous thing happened. Everybody in the airport disappeared. No one else existed for those moments, just Beth and the old man. The love that she felt for him was like nothing she had ever felt before. She knew it was the perfect love of

Love Connection

God emanating from within. It was a moment she didn't want to end. She combed and combed until his hair was as soft and smooth as an infant's.

Then Beth knelt in front of him and asked, "Do you know Jesus?"

"Yes, I do. My bride wouldn't marry me until I knew the Savior," he said. "You see, the problem is, I haven't seen my bride in months. I've had open heart surgery and she's been too ill to come and see me. I was just sitting here thinking to myself what a mess I must be for my bride."[1]

This is the kind of love I am talking about; when you lose all sense of yourself to do a kind act for someone else. When you obey the Spirit of love in you no matter what it takes, that is perfect love. That is the love that changes the world.

> *When you obey the Spirit of love in you no matter what it takes, that is perfect love. That is the love that changes the world.*
>
>

When you live to give love, you are in your setup. Loving is the greatest calling you will ever attempt in life, and it's what God has set you up to do. So you might ask yourself, "Have I done something lately that is similar to what Beth did?" When was the last time you heeded the voice of God from within, and in your obedience, were consumed with the presence of God?

Where love is present, God is there also. You cannot separate the two because God is love.

Beth's reward was far greater than the price she had to pay for it. "Give, and it will be given to you. A good measure, pressed down, shaken together and running over" (Luke 6:38). You always get much more than you give. You're not looking for a return; it's simply a fact—God's sowing and reaping principles stand firm forever. His Word yields a harvest every single time.

Love is transforming. To love is to give life. Giving love to others is the answer to your own need for love. To love and to be loved is the greatest desire in the heart of man.

Do you want to become great? The greatest thing you can do is to love someone unconditionally. Would you like to be highly esteemed and honored by your friends, family, or peers? Give them what they need, without any expectation of return. Do you want people to be blessed by your presence? Esteem others more highly than yourself.

> *Giving love to others is the answer to your own need for love.*
>
>

God is elated when you finally admit you want to be somebody important. We were created in the image of God and God is great. His vision for you is to become a great nation. That means you and your whole family are to be great. He wants our children and grandchildren and all generations after us to become great.

We all want to inherit a good name and leave behind a legacy for our children to follow. We've sat in funeral services of family and friends, thinking about how they lived their lives. We remember all the good things they have done and how they touched our lives with their love.

Then the old familiar thoughts come to mind. "What have I done? Has my life had a positive effect on others? I wonder what they'll say about me when I pass on."

It's good to have a little soul-searching moment in those times, but not to go into depression because of all the things you think you should have done. Instead, use that time in a positive way. Take your thoughts outward instead of inward. Think about whom you can help today. Make a mental list of three things you can do better today.

Love Connection

Put actions to your thoughts. I usually need to write mine down so I won't forget to do them. "The only thing that counts is faith expressing itself through love," (Gal. 5:6). That's when your life counts. That's when you make a difference in your life, family, and relationships.

Tell the people in your life how much you love them. Be creative. Think about how you could show them love in a way they would really get it. My husband feels loved when I tell him how great he is. If I brag on him in front of the kids, he turns red and smiles. That's when I know that I've really touched him with my love.

Live to give love and you will feel loved, too. God loves you back and his perfect love is your reward. "Perfect love casts out fear" (1 John 4:18 NKJV). Life is meant to be spent giving love.

Your setup is all about giving and doing it with purpose. Then your life is meaningful, exhilarating, and fun. You will never wonder if your life will leave a lasting impression on the world. You will never wonder if you have become great. You will know it.

The world is waiting for you to mark it with your love. Your family needs your love more than anything else you could give them. Your friends depend on your love to encourage and help them be successful in life.

Someone in your neighborhood needs your love right now, just to get through the day. Your love has the power to create greatness in this world and in the lives of everyone you know. "Love never fails" (1 Cor. 13:8).

Years ago, there was a woman who worked for us who shared with me a love connection in her life. It was a transforming experience for her. Elizabeth had never felt loved. She always felt rejection when she was in a group of people. She had a very low self-image and never thought that she had anything important to say.

When she got married, she had a hard time believing that her husband really loved her. She always said, "If you really knew me, you wouldn't love me."

You've Been Set Up

Elizabeth did not believe that love could be sincere and unconditional. Even believing that God loved her was a problem. She tried very hard to do everything right to earn the love of others, but it was never enough. In her eyes, she always missed the mark.

Elizabeth's insecurities and fears were the result of not having a father image. Her father was absent most of the time. When he was around, he didn't give her the love and attention that she needed from him. This caused her to feel rejected and abandoned by him, which left her needy and insecure.

Her heavenly Father set her up to conquer this injustice. He looked down from heaven and said, "That's enough. She will no longer have to live in this pain. I have placed someone in her life that will love her with the truth to set her free."

That's when Katy walked into her life. Katy was a Christian and very knowledgeable of the Bible. The two met at church and became great friends.

Katy recognized gifts and talents inside of Elizabeth and began to encourage her in them. The more she encouraged her, the more Elizabeth's heart began to open up and she was able to share her hurts and disappointment.

Katy would pray healing for her broken heart and freedom from her past. Ironically, Katy had been through the same things in her life. Christian friends had helped her conquer her pains and sorrows and now she was strong enough to help Elizabeth.

Katy spent months sowing love and truth into Elizabeth's heart until all the pain was gone. God completely set her free from rejection and restored her self-confidence. The power of unconditional love set Elizabeth's mind, will, and emotions free from the lies she had believed her entire life.

Love Connection

Elizabeth was launched into her setup. The junk in her soul had kept her from doing the things that God had called her to do. Katy's love changed her life.

We have a short time in this life to share our love with the people in our world. Impacting lives with the love of Jesus will always leave a lasting mark. God's love has the power to penetrate into the innermost part of a person's being. We have the power to heal the brokenhearted and to set the captives free.

"Love is the fulfillment of the law" (Rom. 13:10). We don't have to work at doing everything right anymore. All we have to do is love. Love is following God and God will lead us to the right thing.

That "right thing" is your setup. When you are loving God and loving your neighbor as yourself, you are 100 percent in your setup. If you're withholding love, having issues with people, and harboring unforgiveness in your heart, you're not in your setup. I know that is simple and blunt. Truth is blunt.

The greatest person on earth is the one who loves. It's not who you become in this life, but how much you give to others that makes you a great person. The Bible says we are obligated to love others.

"Let no debt remain outstanding, except the continuing debt to love one another, for he who loves his fellowman has fulfilled the law" (Rom. 13:8).

Joe Bayly, a Christian author and minister, had a rebellious son named Tim. Joe tried to reach Tim with arguments and rules, but he still rebelled. Tim eventually left his home, left the faith, and lived a prodigal life in an old house in Chicago. Tim's rebellion broke Joe's heart.

Late one night, Joe got a phone call. "This is the police," the voice on the other end of the line said. "Your son was arrested for a DUI. We have him here in the town jail." Joe got out of bed and drove a half hour to the jail where his son was being held. When he got there, they told him that his son wasn't there. Joe thought he had driven to the wrong place, so he drove to the next town, the next town after that, and the next town after that.

Finally, around four o'clock in the morning, Joe decided to drive to an old house in Chicago where he knew Tim had been sleeping. The door wasn't locked, so he stepped inside and looked for his son. In the faint light of the darkened room, he saw him asleep in a sleeping bag that was strewn across an old mattress. He walked over to the mattress and stood over Tim. Then, moved with compassion, he bent down, lightly kissed Tim on the cheek, and left.

In the months that followed, Tim started visiting his parents. He returned to church and recommitted his life to Christ. He even announced he was going into the ministry. Today, Tim's a Presbyterian pastor in Indiana.

Years later, Joe finally asked Tim what made him want to come back home. Tim looked at his dad and said, "Don't you know? Remember that night years ago, when you got a call that I was in jail? Dad, that was my friend. It was a prank. When you came to the house, I only pretended to be asleep. I was wide awake. I knew you'd driven all night in the cold, and I wondered what you were going to do to me. And all you did was bend down and kiss me on the cheek. Dad, the kiss brought me back."[2]

We have an obligation to love the world and everyone in it. It's payback time. Jesus loved us when we were sinners. Now, we are expected to love others the same way he loved us—unconditionally.

If we sincerely love, we will do no harm to anyone. Because of his Spirit of love in us, we have the ability to love everyone. Draw from the well of love that is in you when you need it. If love never fails, we cannot fail.

In love, you step up to a supernatural realm where God can get your attention and reveal your destiny.

One day, a Pharisee tested Jesus by asking, "Teacher, which is the greatest commandment in the Law?" Jesus replied: "'Love the Lord your God with all your heart and with all your soul and with all your mind.'

This is the first and greatest commandment. And the second is like it: 'Love your neighbor as yourself'" (Matt. 22: 36-39).

The Pharisees were experts of the Law and I'm sure they were asking Jesus which commandment was the most necessary to become great. When they heard his answer, they did not know what to say. They probably went away mad, knowing there was not a shot they could do it.

Under the Law, they were doomed to sin. They didn't have the power of the Holy Spirit to help them overcome and be doers of the Word. They wanted to do what was right but were going about it the wrong way.

Jesus did not rebuke his disciples for wanting to become great. He told them how to do it. He simply told them whoever became the least among them would be the greatest.

Whoever humbles himself and becomes a servant to all will be the greatest. Look away from yourself and your needs and become a servant of love. Live to give.

Begin to look for ways to give. The smallest act of love in your eyes could be the greatest gift of all time to the one who needs it. Never talk yourself out of giving. Act fast when prompted by the Holy Spirit. Don't lean to your own understanding; instead, trust God. His timing is always perfect.

Don't limit yourself in ways to give. Love, like gifts, comes in many different packages. Create your way, freely giving in your own style. When you do, more and more you will discover your original purpose. You will move right into your setup.

CHAPTER NINETEEN

Grace, Amazing Grace

How do men get up and go to work every day to pay the bills and provide for their families? How do moms get up all hours of the night to nurse their newborn babies, then wake up early to take care of their toddlers?

How do doctors, after losing a patient, go back to work with hope and determination? How do schoolteachers walk into a room of rowdy kids, day after day?

It amazes me how starving kids in Ethiopia have smiles on their faces. How low-income families provide food and shelter for the homeless. How the volunteer goes to church to clean the toilets.

Even more personally, how did you get through the death of your loved one? How did you survive the torment of fear? How did you hang on in your hopeless situation? How did you find strength and courage to face that giant in your life?

What makes this happen? There's only one true answer. Grace, amazing grace. God's unlimited power and ability. His power working in you makes all things possible. His grace empowers you with what you need, when you need it. Impossibilities become realities when you are linked with God through divine birth.

You've Been Set Up

You have a partnership with Jesus. He is the head of the church, full of mercy and grace. You are his body, equipped to enforce and release his grace into the earth. You've been set up to be his distributor of goodness and blessing to all those who cross your path in life.

Well-known pastor and author Dutch Sheets was on his way to Guatemala to rebuild shelters after the devastating earthquake of 1976. It had killed thirty thousand people and left a million homeless.

While praying before the trip, the Lord spoke to Dutch's heart very clearly that he was to represent Jesus to the people, being his voice, his hands, and his feet. Doing what he knew Jesus would do if he were there in the flesh.

Dutch realized that God was asking him to be his ambassador. God had given him grace (his power and ability) for the trip. He would go out in the authority of Christ, not his own. Dutch would represent Jesus and the victory of what he had already done at the cross.

For one week, Dutch and his team built shelters during the day and preached the Word to the people at night. The people listened but not many responded to his message of salvation.

On the last day, one of his team members told him what they had found on the far side of the village—a little girl, six years old, tied to a tree like a dog. She was filthy, helpless, and alone.

Not believing what they were seeing, they asked the family that lived there, "Why is this small girl tied to that tree?"

"She is crazy," the parents replied. "We can't control her. She hurts herself and others. She runs away if we turn her loose. There is nothing we can do for her so we have to tie her up."

Dutch immediately knew that he was called there specifically to pray for this little insane girl. This was why God had so clearly spoken to his heart, "Represent me." He had been set up to be the vessel God would use to set this little girl free from her torment.

Grace, Amazing Grace

By faith, Dutch entered into the grace that God had given to him to do God's work. The power of God began to rise up on the inside of him. Dutch thought to himself, "The emphasis is not on me but on the one who sent me. I am simply God's spokesman. I will merely release what he has already done. Jesus has finished the work of delivering this little girl at the cross; my prayers release his work. I'm only a distributor of his grace, what he has already produced."

Yes, God was faithful to his Word. When Dutch prayed for the little girl, she was totally set free and delivered from the tormenting spirit. Witnessing this miracle, the whole village now wanted to know about Jesus. As a result, they all gave their hearts to Christ.[1]

The people in that village saw the evidence of God's grace upon Dutch's life. He stepped out in faith and obeyed; God supplied the power.

There are many wounded and hurting people "tied to trees" around the world. Some may live in your neighborhood or sit beside you at work. Their chains are abuse, addictions, anger, broken dreams, greed, lust, and more. They are waiting for your grace to be poured out to them. In Christ, you have the ability to set them free.

Grace is plentiful in your set-up life. Grace to do amazing things, just like Dutch.

"God is able to make all grace abound to you, so that in all things at all times, having all that you need, you will abound in every good work" (2 Cor. 9:8).

Plan A is for ordinary people, like you and me, to do supernatural things. But first you must wholeheartedly believe in the victory of Calvary. You must be convinced that what Jesus did at the cross is complete and final; that the blood he shed for all mankind has set us free. Then you must rise up in the grace that God has given to you before the beginning of time to represent him, the Victor.

Plan B is to waste the cross; to forfeit the grace of God and walk away from your setup. "The fear of man brings a snare" (Prov. 29:25 NKJV). When we cling to worthless idols, worshipping other things or people instead of God, the grace of God has no value. Your life cannot flow with God, but becomes hard, heavy, and oppressive.

Most Christians live far below their grace level. They are not aware of their God-given abilities. Some feel powerless in hopeless situations, when the power to change that circumstance is already within them. They look to themselves and see weakness, instead of hooking up with the grace of God to provide the miracle.

The apostle Paul boasted in 2 Corinthians 12:9-12 that he delighted in weaknesses, hardships, and trials. For when he was weak or powerless in his own self, he had to depend on God to empower him to overcome. God's grace is always sufficient. He is almighty God on the scene, the one who delivers us from all of our troubles.

Grace is freely available to you at all times. You can't earn grace by being good; you possess an abundant provision of grace because you are a child of God. And God doesn't play favorites. No one has more grace than you. Approach the throne of grace so that you may receive mercy and find grace to help you in your time of need, reassures Hebrews 4:16.

Grace has awarded you with gifts, talents, and abilities. Those things that seem simple and natural to you reveal what flavor of grace has been given to you.

For instance, my friend Cara has the ability to befriend someone in an instant. People are attracted to her like a magnet. She can make a person feel like a million dollars by a few sincere words. She doesn't use flattery; only honest compliments that touch the heart. It's natural for her, a gift of God's grace.

Cara cares. She loves people and people love her. I've watched her influence people for Jesus by her dynamic personality. She continually brings new people to our women's Bible study. Cara is like a shepherd that finds the little lost sheep one at a time.

That's powerful!

Grace also teaches us to say no to ungodliness and worldly passion, to live a self-controlled, upright, and godly life. To be godly, you need grace. Grace saves you from yourself and who your flesh wants to be. Grace has a voice that guides your thoughts and actions.

> *Grace saves you from yourself and who your flesh wants to be.*

Sometimes your flesh doesn't want to cooperate. Things like being humble, having self-control, and loving your enemies sometimes seem unreachable. You know what you should do, but don't think you can or maybe don't want to. That's when you cry out for his amazing grace.

God's grace enables you to do what is right. Train yourself to lean on his power to do what you think is impossible. You can connect to his grace by asking, believing, and receiving. Trust the Creator for what you cannot see.

Ask for grace! Grace to know you're set up. Grace to flow in your life to help others. Grace to help you be godly and make right decisions. Grace to stand up to adversity and run your race with dignity. Grace to love your enemies. It's possible.

Don't forsake the gift of his grace. Access your grace by faith. It's free! You need it every day. By grace, the weak can say, "I am strong," the sick can say, "I am healed," and the poor can say, "I am rich." Whatever you need, his amazing grace is all-sufficient for you.

> *Trust the Creator for what you cannot see.*

Grace overflows into your life when you hang out with God. The more time you spend with him, the more grace you will have. The more grace you embrace, the greater the light will shine from within. The greater the light, the clearer your setup will be.

When I get ugly on the outside, my problem is on the inside. I know I need a good dose of God. Maybe I'll listen to a good teaching or sit alone in my favorite chair with my Bible. Time with God completely changes my heart. When I soak in his grace, my countenance changes from ugly to pretty. My husband says that pretty is so much better.

When I spend time alone with God, I can go from being very upset with someone to wanting to help them, in a matter of minutes. I can be in fear and torment and come out of my time with God as cool as a cucumber. I can be acting like the devil and come out an angel. I can be anxiously confused and come out with the answer.

Why? His amazing grace has changed me. Now I have the mind of Christ. His thoughts, feelings, and expressions have invaded my mind, will, and emotions. Now my spirit man is in charge. My desires are lined up with God's. Now things are in the right order. My will is submissive to his perfect and pleasing will for me.

Man is conditioned his entire life to work hard for his blessings and the right to be successful. He is taught his whole life long to depend upon himself to make things happen, to create success, and to map out his own destiny.

You have been programmed by the world to believe that you are totally responsible for your future. How successful you become in this life is entirely up to you. In other words, you are on your own.

God has a better way and it's the opposite of what the world would tell you. The world says you need to only believe in yourself; God says you need to believe in his amazing grace. You can do your destiny all by

Grace, Amazing Grace

yourself if you want to, but you'll never experience the ultimate setup for your life.

God created you to need him. He wants to have his way in your life. You make the choice—the hard way or his way. You can do it the hard way, all by yourself, if you want to. His plan for your life is far beyond what you could create. His guidance and help are available for your own good.

Challenge yourself to let his amazing grace be in charge of your life. Let go of your simple ways and hop on your Daddy's back. He'll carry you off to adventures you could never imagine. He'll cause you to succeed beyond your natural ability. It is his pleasure to show you the good life and equip you to live it.

Please understand, I'm not saying you don't have to work hard. God expects you to go the extra mile. You will work harder than anyone else, because in God's plan, you will love what you do. According to Ecclesiastes 5:19, blessed is the man that is happy at his work, it is a gift from God.

Your setup is full of work you enjoy. Can you imagine waking up in the morning and wanting to go to work? That's what God wants to lead you into—working and having fun at the same time. You'll love it, it's easy; easy meaning, you ease right into it, you're good at what you do, it comes naturally to you. That's grace.

God set you up to look just like him; gracious, loving, strong, and wise. Just as your children reflect you, you also have been set apart to look like him. When you do, people will be drawn to you. You will have that special look that says, "I'm God's." You will have extreme joy and perfect peace. Just what the world is looking for.

You have heard many times, you become who you hang with. I could always tell who my children were hanging with just by how they would talk when they got home from school. Hang out more with God and you will act just like him. You'll become irresistible. People will want what you have. That's a good thing!

You've Been Set Up

When I was a young mom at home with my kids, I started watching soap operas. The drama was contagious. I got hooked big time. No matter where I was, I would make sure I could watch my show. I would plan my whole day around *The Young and the Restless*.

I didn't realize how much it affected my thinking. I started picturing things happening in my life the way they were on the show. Then one day, while having a heated conversation with my husband, I blurted out the same words that I had heard on the last episode.

They weren't nice.

I couldn't believe I said that. I realized that I was acting out what I had faithfully put in my mind an hour a day for the past year. I was programming my life for destruction.

That was not who I wanted to be. I didn't want to feel that way. That was the end of the soaps for me. Soaps are for dopes!

Isn't it wonderful to learn in Romans 5:20 that where sin abounds, grace abounds all the more! Not that watching soap operas was a sin; of course not. But I was hooked, and I needed grace to walk away and never go back.

The world molds us to be ungodly; the Word molds us to be like God. Consistent with Romans 12:2, we cannot allow ourselves to be conformed to this world. Instead, we are to be transformed by the renewing of our minds by the Word (grace) of God.

Your setup is in the "godly life." God cannot work in the realm that is not his own. You will not find your best life in the world. The world will always bring you trouble. The godly life leads you into wealth and possessions and no trouble comes with it. That's a promise from Proverbs 10:22.

When you spend time with God and in the Word, you desire to do his will. Truth exposes the darkness. The things that steal the grace of God are not so appealing anymore. Little by little, your cravings for other things go

Grace, Amazing Grace

away. You're not looking for the next fix or rush in life. The rush is inside of you.

Your daily life begins to reflect God's love. You want to please him and do right. You know God and where you're going in life. You're not stumbling around in the darkness any longer. Your path is bright. Your course is clear and concise, leading straight to the bull's-eye. You're in your setup and it's exciting.

CHAPTER TWENTY

Crazy Love

Can you imagine God asking a young righteous prophet to marry a prostitute? Well, he did!

Hosea was a young man of God who was waiting for the perfect wife to come into his life. So often, he fantasized about her, dreaming about how beautiful she would be.

A virtuous woman full of compassion and strength. Hosea pictured them having children and how they would raise them up to love and serve the Lord. Together, they would spend their days in happiness and contentment.

But then "the LORD said to him, 'Go, take to yourself an adulterous wife and children of unfaithfulness'" (Hos. 1:2). Can you see the bewildered look on Hosea's face, "Is that you, Lord? What about the beautiful virgin I had in mind?"

But the Scripture doesn't say that he contended with the Lord. Clearly, Hosea did not have a problem hearing from God or obeying him. In the very next verse, Hosea marries Gomer, the prostitute God had chosen for him.

Hosea chose to love Gomer and her illegitimate children unconditionally. He gave them his name, a home, and they became a family.

You've Been Set Up

But Gomer couldn't break free from the habits of her past. One day she packed it up and left. She went back to the lifestyle she was familiar with. Back to the streets.

Gomer was uncomfortable in her healthy home life. She couldn't receive the true love that Hosea offered to her, so she fled.

Again, the Lord spoke to Hosea, instructing him to go find his wife, bring her back, and show love to her again even though she had been unfaithful to him. Hosea could have thought, "What? Shouldn't I divorce her and marry the beautiful virgin? What about *my* feelings?"

No! Hosea did not argue with God. He immediately ran out to find Gomer. He found her at the slave table. "I'll pay whatever you ask, just let me have my wife!" So he bought her back. Never again would she be a prostitute.

Hosea believed that eventually his love would heal the wounds of her past. His love would cover her. Love could not fail to bring wholeness into her heart. Gomer did become whole. Her name means "complete."

The love story between Hosea and Gomer is a perfect picture of God's unconditional love for his children. It doesn't matter how many times you fall away or how horrible your past has been. You could be tangled up in generational sins of your forefathers, trapped by an addiction, helpless to change.

> *You are never too far gone for God.*
>
>

You are never too far gone for God. His love for you is everlasting and unchanging. Allow his love to sink down into your heart to heal your past disappointments, broken dreams, hurts, or pains.

Start believing him for a better life. Expect to live in the setup he has mapped out for you. Don't shrink back and say you don't deserve it. March ahead and leave that garbage behind you. God has amazing things in store for you. He always has success on his mind for you.

When you go about your day, God shows up when you least expect. Yes, he's there all the time, but we're not always paying attention to his interaction.

How many times have you barely missed an accident on the road? Maybe you had to go back to the house to get your cell phone. Or remember the time when, daydreaming, you missed your exit off the freeway? Taking another route, you missed the traffic delay caused by the road construction you weren't aware of. When you do realize what happened, you think, "Oh, thank God! I would have missed my appointment!" Our Father is always taking care of us; we are forever on his mind.

The measure of God's thoughts towards you is endless. You are on his mind all the time, and thinking about you puts a smile on his face. His thoughts for you are for peace. "Peace" in the Old Testament Hebrew is translated as "total prosperity."

His will is for you to be prosperous in every area of your life—spirit, soul, and body. His thoughts toward you are for your total well-being—nothing missing and nothing broken. He is thinking about your life from start to finish and is pleased about what he has created. You have been set up for the good life.

Faith in God's presence and his unfailing love to take care of us is the only way to live. I feel sorry for people who choose not to live in this security. What the future holds for the unbeliever is que será será; whatever will be, will be. But for God's kids, every day is brighter than the day before. There is no trouble in the future of his children!

There is no trouble in God's setup for our lives. Can you believe that? Can you wrap yourself around that truth and never let it go? Can you decide to agree with God so that your life can be blessed?

Just try it for a day. See what happens. What do you have to lose?

Believe in God for one day. Believe that he loves you. Put your hope in his unfailing love for you. Expect his love to heal you and make you whole. Ask for his blessings to come into your life. Ask him to do what you think is impossible. He is ready and willing to act on your behalf. God wants you to need him. He wants to be your Savior. His love will make you complete, just as it did for Gomer.

God's plans for your life are too much! The destiny he has equipped you for is extraordinary. Little by little, he will reveal his thoughts for you as you are able to grasp how blessed he has made your life.

I studied the life of a woman I deeply admired whose name I will call Lucille. She was a woman of virtue and love. She was born into a family of five children. Being the middle child, she was kind of lost in the shuffle. Raised during the depression, she remembered not having shoes to wear to school. Her father was a traveling salesman, and her mother played the role of a parent who loved a favorite child. Unfortunately, Lucille was not it. Consequently, she pretty much raised herself.

Lucille figured out at an early age that when she went to church she was happy. She developed a wonderful relationship with the Lord all on her own. Because her heart was full of his love, she could love others unconditionally. As a result, Lucille was a happy-go-lucky little girl who didn't let her circumstances get the best of her. She always looked on the bright side of things and drew closer and closer to God for love and comfort.

Lucille fell in love and married a marine when she was twenty-seven. She was crazy about him and he loved her. Leo had also been raised in a poor family of five children and lacked parental guidance. His childhood left him curious about the world and it wasn't long before he was looking for happiness in all the wrong places. Leo found himself caught up into a world of drinking, partying, and women. Even though he loved his wife, he felt powerless to overcome his desires for other things.

Lucille had made her marriage vows for better or for worse, and she was going to stick to them. She also was in a denominational church that was her saving grace, and did not want to be excommunicated by divorce. So she stayed in the marriage and Leo continued to live a double life.

Lucille had four children and was a wonderful mom. She was totally devoted to her children and kept a spotless home. She never let on to any of the children why their father was never around. Leo would come home after the children were in bed and left before they got up in the morning.

Lucille would always tell her children what a wonderful father they had, who worked so hard to provide for them. She would compliment him in front of her children, which left them thinking Dad was a pretty great guy. It wasn't until the children became teenagers that they figured out on their own where Dad had been all those years.

How could Lucille hide the truth all those years and why? Lucille had made a commitment to love. She had faith that her husband would always love her and a desire for her children to love him. She was expressing her faith through unconditional love.

Her love was patient, surely was not self-seeking, and kept no record of wrongs. Her love always persevered and always covered her husband. She laid down her life so her children would have a relationship with their dad.

Counselors would have told Lucille to get a divorce and take him to the cleaners. Get all you can from him, he deserves to hurt. Most mothers would have told their children every dirty detail and turned their children away from their father. Lucille was a beautiful woman and could have married again. She could have had a wonderful husband who only had eyes for her. She knew she did not have to put up with abuse and the constant pain of rejection.

Lucille chose what was right for her. Her strongest desire was to keep her family together, to love her husband unconditionally, and to keep her covenant. She was empowered to do that because of the love of God that was in her heart. She was secure and complete in God and her relationship with him.

When her last child got married, she divorced Leo. Leo married again, but was never happy. Lucille stayed single. Leo had a relationship with his children, but Lucille held their highest respect and honor. All of her children are still married and have never divorced. Her children have a relationship with the Lord and continue to grow in his love, thanks to Lucille's example.

She always stayed friends with Leo and never spoke an unkind word about him. Before Leo passed away, Lucille came to his bedside. They looked into each other's eyes, with tears running down both of their cheeks. They held hands and spoke loving words to one another.

The love was still there. Lucille's love did not fail. In the end, she felt his love for her once more. Leo's eyes showed the regret he felt because he hadn't loved her with the same kind of love. Leo had messed up his setup and he knew it.

No rejection, trouble, or persecution can separate you from the love of God. When everyone else around you turns against you, it doesn't matter, because you are secure in God's love. His love for you is really all you need.

Man's love will fail, but God's love is for eternity. *God loves you!* He is crazy in love with you! He loves everything about you! He loves you when you're good and just as much when you're bad.

He loved you when you did that thing that you can never forgive yourself for. He loved you when you willfully sinned and messed your life up. Nothing can change his love for you. It's permanent and forever!

If you would take the time to grasp his love for you, you would never have a need for love and acceptance from anyone else in this world. Imagine being so secure in his love that when people hurt you it doesn't penetrate your soul.

His love is a guard around your heart. You can never be wounded. You will never again be caught up with meaningless issues. You will be filled up to all the fullness of God. Imagine feeling the love that God has in his own heart.

When we act out of the love God put in our hearts, we feel his love. I'm talking about his supernatural love. There is no greater feeling on earth than the warmth of his love.

Love is the key to everything in life. Walking in the light of his love is what moves mountains and opens doors that have been locked for centuries.

When you put God's love into action, nothing can hinder the work of your hands; you are operating in the supernatural realm where dreams become reality. Love is the power that catapults you into your setup so you can fulfill your destiny.

CHAPTER TWENTY-ONE
When Turbulence Hits

Success is failure turned inside out,
The silver tint of the clouds of doubt,
And you never can tell how close you are,
It may be near when it seems so far;
So stick to the fight when you're hardest hit;
It's when things seem worse
That you must not quit. [1]

Too many people acknowledge their mistakes as failures. They give up on their dreams right before they become a reality. They believe thoughts like "I don't know why I thought I could do this" or "I can't take another failure," instead of realizing that mistakes are the process to success. They're too quick to become discouraged and give up.

When your hit the hardest, dig your heels in the solid ground and determine not to quit. The enemy shoots his best shot right

> *Mistakes perfect the dream—the more you make, the greater the outcome.*
>
>

before your breakthrough. Don't be set back by his foolishness, your victory is right around the corner.

Mistakes perfect the dream—the more you make, the greater the outcome. In the face of adversity, you need to persevere. With God on your side, how can you fail? We have a promise that says, "If God is for us, who can be against us?" (Rom. 8:31). You've got to be determined that you can overcome any obstacle in your life with God on your side.

You may not realize it, but what God has put on the inside of you can conquer any giant. When you find yourself in a life-threatening situation, what comes out of you? Who do you trust; yourself or God?

My daughter, Kelli, was on a short flight back to Phoenix with her four children. What was supposed to be ninety minutes, turned into three, grueling, hand-clenching hours.

It was monsoon season in Arizona and storms blow in from out of nowhere. So it was that evening. About twenty minutes away from landing, they hit turbulence. It continuously got worse. The pilot circled around Phoenix for almost an hour, waiting for the storm to pass.

Everyone on the plane was tense. Passengers were nervously talking, wondering what the pilot was going to do. Then the plane took a startling twenty-foot drop. Everyone screamed at once, now on the verge of panic.

The young children sitting behind Kelli were traveling alone. Frightened, they began to cry.

Kelli had already been praying with her children, comforting and assuring them that all would be fine. Now, her prayers were getting louder and louder, so much so that all those around her could hear her pray.

Then she stood up, turned around to the children behind her, and spoke boldly. "You are going to be fine and this plane is going to land safely!"

Unexpectedly, all those around her became calm. Kelli's faith-filled words took authority over the enemy and the overwhelming fear inside that plane. One word spoken in faith brought peace.

When Turbulence Hits

Minutes later, the pilot announced that they were going to land because they were running out of gas. "Prepare yourself for a bumpy ride," he added.

Maybe that was too much information! Just land the plane.

It seemed like it took forever. When the wheels touched ground, everyone cheered for the pilot. Several passengers found Kelli to thank her for praying.

What if Kelli hadn't been praying? What if she hadn't taken dominion over the fear that was so prevalent? I can only imagine the war in the heavenlies when Kelli took her spiritual authority.

The enemy comes in one direction but flees from us in seven when we step up in faith and demand our rights. When we speak to the mountain in the name of Jesus, it has to move. The enemy bows his knee to the name of Jesus. And when we pray according to the Word, God himself watches over his Word to perform it.

As a grandma, I could be tempted to wonder if this terrifying experience would have a negative effect on my grandchildren and leave them with the fear of flying.

On the contrary, faith in their divine connection with Father God and his unfailing love for them became more real than ever. Because of that experience, they are more fully equipped to go through life and be more than conquerors.

We are always victorious in Christ Jesus. His promise to us in Isaiah 54:17 is "No weapon that is formed against thee shall prosper; and every tongue that shall rise against thee in judgment thou shalt condemn. This is the heritage of the servants of the Lord, and their righteousness is of me, saith the Lord" (KJV).

To me, this is one of the greatest promises in the Bible. This Scripture has the power to fill you with courage and hope. The number of times I have used this Word for my own life is countless. Each time it has saved me from destruction.

Find a Scripture like this one to stand on when things get tough. The enemy is a liar, a deceiver, and an accuser. His aim is at you! Be ready with the Word of God to knock him off his feet.

Every day, there are situations that challenge our faith. Many weapons come against our destiny. They come from all different directions and sources.

The Bible warns us to "be sober, be vigilant; because your adversary the devil, as a roaring lion, walketh about, seeking whom he may devour" (1 Peter 5:8 KJV).

I met Talitha when she was seven years old. She was at our church family camp, running around, having fun, playing with all the other kids. One night during a meeting, she ran out of the service and straight to the bathroom. The flu bug hit her hard and she was sick for the remaining days at camp.

After returning home, she didn't get any better, so her parents took her to the doctor. After much testing, they found out that she did not have the flu. Talitha was diagnosed with leukemia.

Talitha had two of the worst strains of cancer. Her doctor said it would be a miracle for her to live six months.

Her parents were prepared spiritually for the battle they had ahead. They were strong Word and faith Christians and knew how to follow the leading of the Holy Spirit. They also had the support of their pastors and many wonderful faith-filled friends.

Talitha's parents depended wholly on the power of the Holy Spirit to lead them in every step of their journey to save their daughter's life. They were ready and willing to do whatever God said. They kept their hearts sensitive to his voice while praying over everything the doctors said and did.

When Turbulence Hits

They took charge and firmly stood on the Word. No weapon formed against Talitha would prosper. They prayed for God to guide them with his Word every day. No matter what the symptoms looked like, they chose to believe by faith that Talitha was healed.

Several times they were told that Talitha would not make it through the night. Praying all night long beside her bed, when the sun came up, she was still alive every time.

Talitha is still alive today; healed and in her setup. Twenty years later, living her life, giving glory to God. No weapon formed against her shall prosper.

Victory is yours when you stand boldly on the Word. The Bible says to do all that you know to do and then stand. The Holy Spirit will give you wisdom to handle every situation. You take action physically, mentally, and spiritually—and then stand firm.

On a trip home from Cancún, our plane had just flown into the clouds when my husband, Dennis, leaned over towards me and said, "I smell smoke. Something is burning." I could tell by the look on his face that he was alarmed.

Quickly, he took my hand and started to pray. "Lord, I thank you that we are supernaturally protected. The blood of Jesus covers us. No weapon formed against us shall prosper. Give this pilot the wisdom of God and the mind of Christ so he can make the right decision at this moment. We fear no evil for you are with us."

About two minutes later, the pilot came on the intercom and announced that we were headed back to Cancún.

"Thank you, Jesus! Get us there before this plane catches on fire!"

Twenty minutes later, we were safely on ground. The flight was cancelled because of wires that were burning. We were rescheduled on a flight for the following day.

You've Been Set Up

> *If fear grips your heart and the obstacles seem overwhelming, know that your victory is right around the corner.*
>
>

What if Dennis had not been alert? What if we didn't know how to pray or just didn't take the time to pray? It could have been doomsday for a lot of people. The good news is God has given us power and dominion over the devil. No weapon formed against us shall prosper.

You need to be way ahead of the devil's game. God will show you ahead of time how the enemy is going to attack. Have a strategy in place to combat whatever he brings your way.

When he accuses you with his lies, speak the Word of truth immediately. Don't give him a second of your attention.

If fear grips your heart and the obstacles seem overwhelming, know that your victory is right around the corner. The enemy always fires his best shot right before your breakthrough. You are a fortified city that cannot be shaken.

Marilyn King, a member of the U.S. Olympic Pentathlon Team, dared to believe she could win a medal in the 1980 Olympics after surviving a car accident that left her flat on her back. The doctors told her to give up her dream because there was no way she could train, as she couldn't even walk.

Marilyn wouldn't accept the obvious; she believed the doctors would be able to treat her and she would get back to her twenty-four-hour-a-day training. She boldly affirmed her belief: "I'm getting better every day and I will place in the top three of the Olympic trials."

With only a few months left, she started training the only way she could, in her head. Marilyn sat for hours in her kitchen chair watching films projected on the wall. She watched for hundreds of hours, studying

When Turbulence Hits

and absorbing. Then she would lay on the couch, visualizing the experience of competing in minute detail. She trained as hard as she could without ever moving a muscle.

Marilyn believed with all of her heart that she could place in the top three at the Olympic trials. By the time the trials actually rolled around, she was healed just enough to compete.

She moved through her five events as if in a dream. Afterwards, as she was walking across the field, she heard a voice on the loudspeaker announce, "Second place, 1980 Olympic Pentathlon: Marilyn King."[2]

Marilyn didn't give up when the odds were against her. She found a way to push forward towards her goal when it seemed impossible. The weapon formed against her was a car accident. She overcame it with faith and a can-do attitude. What is the weapon facing you?

Sometimes the weapon against us is our own free will. We just don't want to do what God asks of us. Jonah of the Bible didn't want to fulfill the call of God for his life. He chose to do his own thing, but God intervened.

God asked Jonah to go to the land of Nineveh to preach the Word. He was to warn the people of their wickedness so they would turn their hearts to God for forgiveness.

Jonah knew that God was merciful and would forgive their sins if they repented. But Jonah did not want God to show mercy to them because they were his enemies. He wanted them to be destroyed.

Jonah had a mandate from God but he chose not to do it. He ran away from God and got on a boat going where he wanted to go. Jonah went as far as he could go in the opposite direction of his purpose and destiny.

Can you imagine God asking you to do something for him and you saying no? Silly question. We've all done that!

While on the boat, a huge storm arose. Jonah, feeling guilty, told his mates to throw him overboard so the sea would become calm. Otherwise, all of them would be destroyed. So they threw Jonah out to sea and he was swallowed by a whale.

Now, inside of the huge fish, Jonah wanted God's attention.

"As my life was slipping away, I remembered the Lord" (Jonah 2:7 NLT).

Inside the fish, on the verge of death, Jonah cried out to God. The forgiving and merciful Lord heard his cry and came to his rescue, as much as to say, "Jonah, I will give you another chance." So God spoke to the fish and it vomited Jonah out onto the dry ground.

The Lord told Jonah a second time to go preach repentance to the people of Nineveh, informing them they would be destroyed in forty days unless they repented.

This time Jonah went. The king of Nineveh listened to Jonah and proclaimed a fast throughout the land. As a result, God turned away from destroying them. But Jonah was not happy. He was so upset he wanted to die. Jonah's ministry had saved one hundred twenty thousand people that he still considered his enemies.

God set Jonah up to do his will in spite of Jonah's mishandling of his own free will. Even when we want to do our own thing, God has a way of changing our minds. He will even use a whale if he has to.

No weapon formed against you shall prosper.

CHAPTER TWENTY-TWO

A Familiar Voice

I'll never forget the morning when the Lord called me to teach the Word. I was sitting in my favorite chair, it was still dark, and I had just finished my daily devotionals. I was silently enjoying the presence of the Lord.

All at once, I heard his voice speak to me, "I'm calling you to teach women." It wasn't an audible voice, although I would love to hear the Lord's voice. It was a still, small voice that came out of my spirit.

At first I thought, "That's not God. He would never ask me to do that because I would never do it. I would never ever get up in front of people to do anything. What a crazy thought!" I took that thought captive and cast it out of my mind.

As I was going about my day, packing lunches and getting the kids off to school, that crazy thought flew through my mind again. This time he said, "I want you to teach women."

Now that really scared me so I immediately spoke out loud and said, "No! I can't and I won't do that!"

I contemplated volunteering more often in the women's ministry; that would make God happy and he would get off my back about teaching. "Good! That's the answer," I told myself, adding, "now go do the laundry!"

You've Been Set Up

Midafternoon, I received a phone call from one of the leaders in the women's ministry. I wondered why she was calling me. She got right to the point. "Would you give a testimony during the offering time at the Bible study?"

All of a sudden, I broke out in a cold sweat. My heart fell to my knees and I started to shake. "I'm sorry, I can't do that. I mean, I'm too shy to get up and talk in front of people."

Then she said she felt like God told her to ask me. I again said I was sorry and she would have to find someone else.

The next morning I realized that I had many notes I had written throughout the years. My notes looked like I could take them into a classroom and teach. I hadn't realized that God had been preparing me for something more, but I still fought off the idea of ever teaching.

A few weeks later, the call came again: "Would you give a testimony at the women's Bible study?"

This time I said I would pray about it. I actually put off praying for a few days, as long as I could. I knew when I prayed, God would say, "Go do it!"

I gave up. I had to obey God. God wanted me to deal with the fear inside of me and I had to submit to his will for my life. I had to trust that he knew what was best for me.

I memorized my testimony and went over it one hundred times a day. I could say it in my sleep. I was dreading the day to come. I even picked up the phone to call and tell them I was sick, when God spoke to my heart again. "Fear not, for I am with you."

"OK! You better be!"

I couldn't believe I did it. I got through the testimony that day with trembling hands and a shaky voice, but I did it. Many testimonies later, guess what happened! Yes, they asked me to teach the Bible study.

A Familiar Voice

Little by little, I conquered the fear of speaking in public. I found out that the thing I feared the most was the thing I enjoyed the most. After many years of teaching, it's still one of my greatest joys.

God's living word for me gave me the courage and power to face the giant of fear. His words "Fear not, for I am with you" were all I needed to conquer the fear in my heart, so I would not miss God's will for my life.

That is the power of the rhema word, the miracle power of God that brings the supernatural into your life. Only that word could change me; I couldn't change myself.

God's spoken word to you will change your life. You'll never be the same. You will begin a generational blessing, passing your spiritual inheritance down to your children and grandchildren, to a thousand generations.

Any pain you go through to establish a blessing is worth it. Today, my daughter is teaching a women's Bible study and my granddaughter who is ten years old thinks nothing of getting up in front of thousands to dance or sing a solo.

Because of God's rhema word to me about not being afraid to teach, instead of a generational curse, my family has a generational blessing going on. God is so good!

Any pain you go through to establish a blessing is worth it.

"It is written, 'Man shall not live by bread alone, but by every word that proceeds from the mouth of God'" (Matt. 4:4 NKJV).

God is speaking to you when you read the Bible and the letters seemed to jump right off the page—you can't seem to read on, you keep going back to the same Scripture, you know that God is trying to get through to you.

He is enlightening your heart by giving to you a living word. This is what we refer to as a "rhema" word. According to Matthew 4:4, man lives by every rhema word that proceeds from the mouth of God.

God wants to speak personally to you every day. He has living rhema word, the fresh bread of life, for you to live on each day. The more rhema words you allow God to reveal to you, the more you will operate in the supernatural realm. Remember, even though we live in this natural world, God has made a way for his kids to live in the supernatural!

> *The more rhema words you allow God to reveal to you, the more you will operate in the supernatural realm.*
>
>

A few years ago, I purchased an Apple computer. The first time I went into the Apple store, I was overwhelmed. I felt like an alien, in a place I didn't belong. (Where was I when modern technology created all these things?) What kind of language were the store employees speaking? I couldn't answer their questions because I didn't know what they were saying. I thought, "This is too much for me, I really don't need all this."

All of a sudden, I heard that voice again. "You need this. Buy it." I wanted to argue but I knew better than that, so I bought the computer. I was relieved to find out that the store offered computer lessons, for people just like me.

After many one-on-one training sessions, I was feeling pretty savvy on my computer. Now I love all the great things my computer can do for me. I did need it, and God talked me into it. He was setting me up to do my heart's desire. Now, I can use it to its maximum potential; it's not just a foreign object.

Getting to know God works the same way. You spend the time to know what he's all about. To become intimate with God, you need to spend time building a close relationship.

A Familiar Voice

It's no different than the relationship you build with your spouse or close friend. You spend time to really get to know everything about them. You invest the energy to know that person inside and out. Every little detail about them becomes important to you.

The closer you become, the greater level of trust and admiration you feel. You become secure in knowing that you could let down the barriers to your soul and be the real you.

It won't take you long to find out that everything about God is amazing and beyond comprehension. The more time you spend with him, the more you depend on him for every little detail in your life. You are one with him, and his will is your only desire.

"For in him we live and move and have our being" (Acts 17:28).

He is the source of your life. You live in the reality that the two of you became one. Nothing can separate that union; you have been grafted together. He is the Vine and you are the branch.

Intimacy with God is not a religious experience and is definitely not being in a prayer closet six hours a day. It is simply a continuous awareness of his presence, delighting oneself in the Lord, with a willingness to know his ways and do his will.

"Cause me to hear thy lovingkindness in the morning; for in thee do I trust: cause me to know the way wherein I should walk; for I lift up my soul unto thee" (Ps. 143:8 KJV).

When the Israelites were wandering in the desert, every morning God provided fresh manna from heaven for them to eat. It was their bread of life. Even though it was just a wafer of bread, it contained all the nutrition they needed to sustain them.

God wants to speak to you before you start your day. He wants to fill you up with his wisdom for the things that are in your day. He wants to prepare you to live out your day in victory.

You've Been Set Up

When we send our children off to school in the morning, we give them all kinds of instructions for their day: "Pay attention to your teacher, be a good friend, eat all your lunch, don't miss the bus, and have a good day!"

You encourage them to do their best. You let them know you will be praying for them to do well on their tests. You want your children to have a great day and feel good about themselves. You equip them for success.

God wants to set us up to have a great day, too. He knows the day that he has planned out for you and wants to give you instructions and encouragement so you will succeed. He wants to fill you up with power to be more than a conqueror.

"I am the vine; you are the branches. If a man remains in me and I in him, he will bear much fruit; apart from me you can do nothing. If you remain in me and my words remain in you, ask whatever you wish, and it will be given you. This is to my Father's glory, that you bear much fruit" (John 15:5, 7-8).

CHAPTER TWENTY-THREE

The Passion Play

Live your life with passion. Adding a little zest to any task will increase your enthusiasm. Get lively! Smile while you're working—it makes your brain think more creatively. A little smile can turn you on to something great.

Take a moment to find out what generates passion in you. What turns you on and makes you light up inside? What causes you to be extravagant? I've often been told that I am extravagant. At first, I didn't take it as a compliment. Then I realized that I just normally think outside of the box. That's what makes me go the extra mile and do extravagant things.

Get in touch with what you love about your life. What is it that you would never want to live without? Even the most negative person has at least one thing they like about their life. Even a person who says they hate their life and everyone in it, loves their dog. They're passionately in love with their dog and he gets all their attention.

Find out what ruffles your feathers, gets under your skin. Something you are compelled to fix, no matter how long it takes.

> *Adding a little zest to any task will increase your enthusiasm.*
>
>

Whatever causes these strong feelings, these compelling emotions of love or hate in you, you need to discover. Your passion is the clue to your setup!

There was a time in my life when I was unusually passionate about what I was doing. So much so that I felt like I was walking in God's footsteps. I could actually feel his heart beat in mine as I followed his leading. I was in my setup.

My daughter-in-law, Juliane, shared with me that she had been praying for her mom's home to be awarded a makeover by *Extreme Makeover*. Juliane had sent a letter with a video and was patiently waiting for a response.

Her widowed mother had lived in her home for twenty-five years and it was in dire need of everything. Her husband had passed away, leaving her a small amount of money. Just paying the mortgage was a stretch.

Many months had gone by with no answer from the *Extreme Makeover* show. Then one morning to my surprise, the Lord spoke to my heart, "You do the makeover!"

"What? Is that you, Lord?"

"Yes! You know my voice. I said *you* do it!"

"How in the world could I do it?"

"Do what they do! You can do all things. I am with you!"

With those words came the fire of God. I felt like my spirit man woke up, stood up, and started to run. Those words spoken right to my heart ignited me with supernatural power and passion!

I knew without a doubt, right then the Spirit of God came upon me and infused me with the ability to do what he asked me to do.

Immediately, I sat down with pen and paper and drew up the plan, as God spoke to my heart. In minutes, God showed me who I needed on the team, how to get the supplies, and how we would get it done.

I couldn't wait to get started! Passion was ablaze in me.

The Passion Play

Within weeks, we had formed a nonprofit organization called The Restoration Foundation. Our motto was "Live to Give."

Everyone was on board. The people God showed me to be on the team all said yes. They were willing to work every weekend on this house.

Juliane and I hit the streets every Friday, calling on businesses and asking for donations. No one could say no to us; we had favor with everyone. We successfully got all the supplies donated from local businesses. One company donated twenty-five thousand dollars' worth of cabinets for the kitchen and bath. We were walking in our setup.

The fire never left my heart. It was one of the most exciting experiences of my life. I couldn't wait till the weekends to work on the house.

In one year, we had successfully rebuilt her mother's entire home. She had the best of the best. To furnish the home, we organized a golf tournament and raised ten thousand dollars. Everything we set our hands to prospered.

It was the easiest thing I've ever been a part of. Juliane's dream had come true. Her mom had a completely brand-new home from top to bottom, including all new furniture, landscaping, and a gourmet barbecue grill. God gave her the desire of her heart. I was actually sad when the project was done. We had witnessed God move in miraculous ways in the hearts of people who "live to give."

The whole project was completed by the power that is in passion. God gave the purpose and supplied me with the passion to do it. Now I can look back and see how he set up the entire project. I already had everything in my life to make it happen.

All the players had been set in place in my life to make it happen. It was easy because it was God's idea, not mine. The passion in my heart attracted people to give, to help, to advise, to be whatever I needed at any moment. Seeing God move on the hearts of the people to give with no expectation of return was life changing for me.

> *The purpose of life is to passionately live a life of purpose.*
>
>

The purpose God has for you is beyond what you can do. It will always involve serving others and working with others. We are all in this world together and support each other's purpose.

The purpose of life is to passionately live a life of purpose. Get excited about finding your purpose and doing it. Take time to ask God for his input. He has a master plan for your life. Most of us get too busy doing our own thing in life and miss out on the God thing.

Start acting like your life counts. Put on the attitude of being a child of almighty God. You have been born into a royal family with a royal purpose.

Expect God to talk to you the same way he talked to me and asked me to do what I thought was impossible. When he gives you something to do, do it knowing that he set you up for success. Step out to do his will, and God will show up and show off his power.

When you're passionate about life, you will step out and live by faith. You will not only believe that God has set you up with purpose, but with passion, and your actions will follow.

You need to step out into the unknown, knowing God is with you and will cause all things to work together for your good. Remember, he is the one who created the universe. He set the stars in the sky and outlined the borders of the sea.

His power holds together our world and everything in it. Setting you up to fulfill your passion in life is a piece of cake for him. Rest yourself in his ability, not your own. When you do, his greatness will shine through your life.

CHAPTER TWENTY-FOUR
Your Best Is Yet to Come

Looking back, how many times have you said to yourself, "If I only knew then what I know today, I would have done things differently? I would have raised my kids differently. I would have run my business differently. I would have never dated that person. I would have kept my mouth shut.

"If I had it to do over, I would have focused more on family and relationships. I would have left bigger tips. I would have been more confident. I would have said I love you more often."

The list of things you wouldn't have done is even more painful. "I wouldn't have let fear keep me back from doing the things I wanted to do. I wouldn't have listened to negative people who influenced my life. I wouldn't have wasted so much time doing nothing. I wouldn't have given in to that addiction. I wouldn't have…

"I would have been so different!"

Yes, you would have. The majority of honest people wish they had another chance to do things bigger, better, and smarter. But, who says you can't have another chance?

You've Been Set Up

Why are you convinced that you are too old or too tired to start all over again? If you are approaching sixty, your life is only halfway there. You can live to be one hundred twenty, according to Genesis 6:3, if you want to.

Before Genesis 6:3, people lived to be hundreds of years old. Some time later, the life span decreased to about one hundred twenty years. By the time the Psalms were written, the average life span was considerably less than seventy years.

That was over three thousand years ago. Today, because of medical and nutritional knowledge, we can live to be one hundred twenty years, if we really take care of ourselves. God's desire is for you to be fully satisfied with a long, healthy life here on earth.

Psalm 91:16 says, "With long life will I satisfy him and show him my salvation."

God is in the business of saving you from death and destruction. It is not his will that anyone die young and dissatisfied. Many do, but it's never because of God. God mourns when his children do not fulfill the number of their days on earth. His will is that we prosper and be in health even as our soul prospers, as stated in the second verse of 3 John.

Old age is a mental attitude, a matter of the mind. If you don't mind, it doesn't matter. People shudder when you discuss old age. Next to the subject of death, it is mankind's least favorite topic.

People try to postpone old age in many ways. They try various products to keep looking and feeling young. Plastic surgery is the fastest growing business in America. People try traveling to relieve boredom, giving them a sense of fulfillment.

Sadly, some of the most miserable people in the world are the aged. As some people get older, they become cantankerous and obnoxious. Their youth is no longer there to protect them or excuse them from bad behavior. They are seen for what their souls really are, without the camouflage of youth.

According to God's plan, the older you grow as a believer, the more you increase in every area of your life. You can have promise, productivity, vitality, confidence, and a great deal of happiness. You can do the things you always wanted to do with excitement and excellence. Your last years can be the crowning glory of your lifetime.

Moses began to sense his responsibility to Israel and to the Lord when he was about forty years old. After spending forty more years in training, he became leader of the people of Israel. It was during his years from eighty to one hundred twenty that he did his greatest work.

James Strom Thurmond was an American politician who served as governor of South Carolina and as a United States senator. He left office at age one hundred as the oldest-serving U.S. senator in history.

Irving Berlin, one of the most successful and prolific musicians and lyricists in history, composed over three thousand songs including, "God Bless America," "White Christmas," "Anything You Can Do," and "There's No Business Like Show Business." He also composed seventeen film scores and twenty-one Broadway scores. Berlin died at age one hundred one.

Bob Hope was an English-born American entertainer who appeared in vaudeville, on Broadway, on radio and television, in movies, and in performing tours for U.S. military personnel. He was well-known for his good-natured humor and the longevity of his career.

As well as commercial work, Hope performed over sixty USO shows across half a century, entertaining troops during World War II, the Korean War, the Vietnam War, and the Gulf War. Hope died at age one hundred.

"The Lord blessed the latter part of Job's life more than the first. He had fourteen thousand sheep, six thousand camels, a thousand yoke of oxen and a thousand donkeys. And he also had seven sons and three daughters. The first daughter he named Jemimah, the second Keziah and the third Keren-Happuch. Nowhere in all the land were there found women as beautiful as Job's daughters, and their father granted them an inheritance along with their brothers. After this, Job lived a hundred and forty years; he saw his children and their children to the fourth generation. And so he died, old and full of years." (Job 42:12-17)

Living in your set up, as advance in years, you advance in all areas of your life. Increasing in every way, your relationships thrive and you are physically whole, mentally smarter, spiritually mature and financially loaded.

This is God's plan for you, to possess the land of too much. Everything your hands touch prospers. Your setup is to live out your days exploiting his glory, where everyone can see that you are extremely blessed.

Billy Graham once said, "Being a Christian is more than just an instantaneous conversion—it is a daily process whereby you grow to be more and more like Christ." You have a promise in Philippians 1:6 that God will complete the work he began in you. God is completely capable of advancing you in his design. Little by little, he is molding you to look like him.

Men can look forward to becoming like the elderly men characterized in Titus 1 as healthy minded, alert, sharp, Christlike in character, masters of the details of life, temperate, sound in faith, holders of spiritually healthy doctrine, and free from sins such as bitterness, envy, and hostility. They are older men who love and encourage others.

Women can look forward to becoming like the older women characterized in Titus 2 as those whose shining inner beauty reflects the glory of God. They are not false accusers or guilty of maligning, evil speaking, or gossip, and they are not vindictive. They are also temperate, skillful, and wise. They have the willing attention of younger women and teach them to be healthy minded, emotionally stable, sound in judgment, poised, in control of themselves, thoughtful of others, free from carnality(chaste), and responsive to their husbands.

When you think you've already done it all, get ready. God doesn't offer retirement in the Bible. To withdraw from an active, productive lifestyle is not in his plan for you.

Our close friend Pete was counting down the days to retirement. He had worked hard his whole life to build his own business and now he was selling it. He was ready to sit back, kick his feet up, and relax.

"This is the life!" he reveled. "No schedule, no one to make accountable, no work!" For six months, Pete played golf, traveled to Europe, visited his out-of-state grandchildren, and watched TV. Everything was great. He was a happy guy.

Approaching his retirement's one-year anniversary, Pete started to get restless. He decided to stop in to see how the new owners of his business were doing. Walking up to the front door put a lump in his throat. Surprisingly, seeing someone sitting at his desk made him depressed. The entire visit made him heartsick.

The next morning, Pete woke up irritated, grumpy, and restless. "What's the deal? Why aren't I happy? I'm retired. This is the good life," he mused. Pete kept telling himself that he was being foolish. For days, he denied his feelings and kept himself busy doing meaningless things.

The feeling of loss grew each day. He regretted selling his business. He felt useless and without a sense of purpose in life. "Why does the grass look greener on the other side of the fence? Why do I miss it? What do I do with my life now?" he pondered.

Maybe you're not at retirement age yet and can't relate to this story. This predicament comes as a surprise-awakening to a lot of people. Retirement is a one-way trip to insignificance.

Retirement—the way the world views it—is not what it is cracked up to be. No longer feeling purposeful, many lose the will to live and die before their appointed time. But God's way is to retire from one adventure to the next.

Just when you think you can't do any more, he gives you a whole new idea. One that won't escape you until you do it. He keeps stretching you and stretching you. When you can't comprehend how it's all going to happen, just remember that God has it all under control.

There's no limit to your potential, whether you are twenty, sixty or ninety. Daniel 12:13 records that Daniel was told to keep on going until the end. At this point, Daniel was in his nineties.

Michelangelo was still designing churches at eighty-eight. Peter Roget was updating his famous thesaurus when he died at ninety. Leo Tolstoy learned to ride a bicycle at sixty-seven and wrote "I Cannot Be Silent" at eighty-two. Alexander Graham Bell was still inventing a year before his death at seventy-five. Thomas Edison produced the telephone at eighty-four. Benjamin Franklin helped the writing of the United States Constitution when he was eighty-one. Frank Lloyd Wright designed the Marin County Civic Center in California at eighty-eight. Pablo Casals was playing the cello at ninety-six and George Bernard Shaw was writing plays at ninety-one. At one hundred, Grandma Moses was still painting pictures.

What did all these people have in common? Why didn't they retire at fifty-five and just take it easy? I believe they all had vision. That vision gave them a reason to live and to give. It gave them purpose. Purpose gives us a reason to live. They were in their setup, living life to the fullest, doing the will of God.

I've got new for you: God has your life planned out from beginning to end. He is your Alpha and Omega. When you continue to live in the abundant life God has planned for all of your days, your last years on earth will be filled with great joy and peace. You will have a keen awareness of the presence of God. You will find his love for you in all the wonders of life. Your level of trusting him will be an unwavering one.

Your relationships will be fulfilling and meaningful. Your capacity to love and be loved will be exceedingly great. Your life will be a witness of his glory.

"The righteous will flourish like a palm tree, they will grow like a cedar of Lebanon; planted in the house of the Lord, they will flourish in the courts of our God. They will still bear fruit in old age, they will stay fresh and green" (Ps. 92:12-14).

CHAPTER TWENTY-FIVE
The Greatest Setup

There is someone who knows you better than you know yourself. This person has the keys to your happiness in life here and now. He is the one and only guarantee of eternal life in heaven. He is Lord of heaven and earth, the one I've talked about throughout this book.

God's only son, Jesus, lived the greatest setup of all time. He was born into this world to die for you. His destiny was to free all of mankind from hell and death.

By taking the sins of the whole world upon himself, his death paid the penalty once and for all. Jesus set you free to be who he has made you to be.

Jesus set you up to be a child of God and heir of every blessing. As his child, you have covenant rights to all the promises of God. Whatever belongs to God belongs to you. You've been set up to live the good life, full of blessing and prosperity.

You must know him intimately by asking him to live inside your heart. He is your Savior and the author of your setup on this earth. He holds the keys to your divine destiny.

You've Been Set Up

If you desire to become a child of God and live out your set-up life, pray this simple prayer of salvation. This is the most important decision you will ever make. Pray it out loud and mean it in your heart and you will be saved.

"Lord Jesus, I desire for you to come into my heart to be my Lord and Savior. Thank you for shedding your blood on the cross for me for the forgiveness of all my sins. I believe that you died on the cross, were resurrected from the dead, and now sit at the right hand of your Father in heaven. Thank you that now I am your child and heir of all that belongs to you. Fill me with your Holy Spirit to overflowing. In your name I pray. Amen."

Congratulations! You are a child of God. The Spirit of the Lord lives in your spirit. You have the power of almighty God living on the inside of you. Now, you can step up with him and live in your setup!

NOTES

Chapter One
1. *Hybrid Mom Magazine,* "Charmed I'm Sure" by Beth Smith, http://www.hybridmom.com.
2. *Woodrow Kroll* (Lincoln, NE: Back to the Bible).

Chapter Four
1. Global-Net Productions-Michael Lienau's Story, http://www.globalnetproductions.com/mshsurvival.html (accessed July 13, 2009).

Chapter Eight
1. AHA Jokes.com.
2. Love Story of Hollis Maynell, http://www.greetinggrams.com/lovestory.htm (accessed July 2, 2009).

Chapter Twelve
1. Pacific Palisades High School, http://www.TruthOrFiction.com (accessed July 2, 2009).

Chapter Eighteen
1. The Beth Moore Hairbrush Story, http://www.fertilethoughts.com/forums/archive.
2. Joe Bayly story, http://www.preachingtoday.com.

Chapter Nineteen
1. Julia Loren and Bill Johnson, *True Stories of Heaven Invading Earth* (2008).

Chapter Twenty-One
1. "Success Is Failure Turned Inside Out" poem, Author Unknown.
2. Marilyn King Olympian Thinking, http://www.thelearningweb.net.

AUTHOR CONTACT INFORMATION

To purchase books, for more information,
or to schedule Mary June Collins to speak,
please contact:
Mary June Collins
maryjunec23@yahoo.com